98-21-2

THE STORY OF THE HEISMAN AND THE MICHIGAN MAN

BY MARTIN JOHN GALLAGHER

98-HARMON   2-WOODSON

4-HARBAUGH   86-WESTFALL

9-FRANKLIN   7-LEACH   41-LYTLE   87-KRAMER

1-EDWARDS   **21-HOWARD**   40-JOHNSON

45-DALEY   23-PERRY   1-CARTER

49-CHAPPUIS   20-HART   5-BELL

6-WHEATLEY   21-BIAKABUTUKA

16-ROBINSON   28-TIMBERLAKE

ACKNOWLEDGEMENTS

All pictures are courtesy of the Bentley Historical Library, University of Michigan unless otherwise noted:

Bentley Historical Library
1150 Beal Ave.
University of Michigan
Ann Arbor, MI 48109-2113

Like the program and players outlined in this work, the Bentley Library is an amazing institution that reflects the spirit of innovation and excellence that defines the University of Michigan. Thank you to the staff members and volunteers that make this information available to us all each and every day.

DEDICATION

I dedicate this book to my loving wife Jennell and parents, who know my blood runs blue. I had a wonderful childhood growing up as one of five children, and spent some very impressionable years in Ann Arbor, Michigan while my father was an ROTC Instructor. I went to games, met players, and could see the Goodyear Blimp circling the Big House from our backyard. My Dad and I have always been Michigan fans, and it is a unique layer of our amazing bond. He knew Bo Schembechler and is a Michigan football historian. I am one of five, no one kid was loved more than the other, but on Saturdays there are two men, 916.69 miles apart, dressed in blue, and hoping for the best. I guess we are two of "those guys" entirely too emotionally invested in the results of a competition between eighteen and twenty year olds, but I wouldn't have it any other way. My wife is an angel, she couldn't tell you a single player's name other than Denard, but come Saturdays in the fall, there she is making food and entertaining friends and relatives in support of my blue blood. I love you all. To true Michigan fans, I hope this book conjures the memories of this great program, and elevates the excitement of the restoration of Michigan Football in the years to come.

GO BLUE!

TABLE OF CONTENTS

1

MICHIGAN AND THE HEISMAN

The University of Michigan has a rich and storied tradition. It is a highly regarded Academic Institution with a history of great football. The Wolverines have been playing football since 1879, and have experienced highs and lows through the one hundred and thirty two years. This book will outline some of the highs, and the three University of Michigan football players who have been awarded the most prestigious individual award in College Athletics, The Heisman Memorial Trophy. It also covers those who came close.

Before we get to the Heisman Memorial Trophy, let me tell you there was even an award prior to the Heisman's creation that made it to Ann Arbor. In 1932, Harry Newman was declared the Nation's Most Outstanding Player, and received the Douglas

Fairbank's Trophy while leading Michigan to a National Championship. Like the Douglas Fairbank's Trophy, the Heisman Memorial Trophy is awarded to the most outstanding College Football player annually, and has been since 1935. The trophy was originally awarded as the Downtown Athletic Club (DAC) Trophy in 1935 to Jay Berwanger, from the University of Chicago. The trophy itself is formed as a work of art is formed, through a process called bronze medal molding. It is approximately fourteen inches long, thirteen and a half inches tall, and weighs around twenty-five pounds. It is awarded to the nation's most outstanding college player, "whose performance best exhibits the pursuit of excellence with integrity." (Heisman.com) It was originally awarded at the DAC, after the completion of the College Football regular season. After the death of John Heisman in 1936, who served as the Director of Athletics at the DAC, the trophy was renamed the Heisman Memorial Trophy. The award continued to be awarded by the DAC from inception to 2001. Then by the Yale Club from 2002-2003, and by the Heisman Trust from 2004 to today.

The Downtown Athletic Club's facilities were damaged following the 9/11 attacks on America. In addition to the countless loved ones and heroes lost in the aftermath of those senseless attacks based on a jealous hatred, they even took a shot at this great sport. It makes me sick deep in my stomach. To those who lost so much on that day, my thoughts will forever go out to you. Following that venue change, the banquet has been hosted at several sites, and most recently at the Nokia Theater in Times Square.

But like America, the tradition of the award lives on. Those who win the award enter an amazing group of football players past and present. Their names are forever entrenched in the history of College Football as well as the minds of College Football fans. The signature plays, the amazing stats, and even the opinions of these great players are broadcast today across the College Football world. The Heisman Memorial Trophy is an individual award. It recognizes one player, from one team, across the United States. In a sport where teamwork, anything but individual schemes, and twenty two student athletes are on the field on every given play, this award is given to one.

College Football coaches search the nation high and low to find the next great players, as well as the others required to fill eighty-five scholarship spots per year. They are allowed to offer up to twenty-five scholarships prior to a season. There are one hundred and twenty teams currently in the highest level of College Football, the Football Bowl Championship Series (FBCS). So if you look at scholarship players alone, if every school has a full roster, the Heisman is awarded to one individual out of 10,200 FBCS players. Of the 10,200, these players distinguished themselves enough in their high school careers to receive an athletic scholarship and college education. With all of that talent to choose from, the Heisman Memorial Trophy is given to only one. It is a rare, prestigious, and sought after award. Yes the odds are better than winning something in the lottery at times. In North Carolina, where I live, you have a have a 1/12,000 chance of winning five hundred dollars in the "Fifty Thousand Dollar Jackpot Game." Unlike the lottery however, this one player annually has the ability to influence the results. They work harder than others and elevate their own play as well as that of their teammates. This individual is able to display enough to be recognized as a Heisman Memorial Trophy winner. Historically, the Heisman is mostly awarded to individuals on highly successful teams despite being an individual award. The Heisman has only been awarded to **_ONE_** player on a losing team in its' storied history. In 1956, Paul Hornung won the Heisman Memorial Trophy. He did even though he played on a 2-8 Notre Dame team. Despite being an individual award, it is certainly correlated to team success. Throughout the history of the award, 13 times the winner's team has also won the National Championship, to include Cameron Newton of Auburn in 2010, and Charles Woodson of Michigan in 1997.

Along with that thinking, anyone who has ever played a down of football, from Pop Warner to the NFL can tell you that football is not an individual sport. You can run like Carl Lewis, hit like Stone Cold Steve Austin, or kick like Pele, but if there aren't others helping you rarely will you achieve success. Football is about matchups and team execution. Those without the ball are in a constant battle, tackling or blocking, trying to create space or eliminate it for the one player who has the ball. It is violent and fluid on each and every play. So despite the fact that it is an individual award, it is also an indicator of team success and the special players who helped to create it.

I could write fifty pages on the award itself, but that is not exactly what this book is about. This is about the University of Michigan, and its' storied history with the Heisman Memorial Trophy. Despite the amazing significance of the award, the University of Michigan *does not, has not, and will not* see the Heisman Trophy as a goal in any given season. The goals are simple at this proud university. In the College Football world before the Bowl Championship Series (BCS), Michigan players knew the goals:

BEAT OHIO STATE

WIN THE BIG TEN

WIN THE ROSE BOWL

The order is debatable, but the message was clear. The modern era of College Football at Michigan calls for BEAT OHIO STATE, win the Big Ten Championship, with the third being the BCS National Championship. Nowhere in these team goals do you see the Heisman Memorial Trophy.

With the media resources of today, the award has become a key piece in the development of a College Football program. The winner is chosen by vote. This great country wouldn't have it any other way. The voters are a combination of key media sources, as well as former Heisman Trophy winners. Programs have and will see the Heisman Memorial Trophy as a goal outside of Ann Arbor, not just aspiring players. This goal is as lofty as the National Championship for the fortunate teams with players talented and distinguished enough to be in the running. Campaigns are launched including emails, mailings, and other media in order to promote candidates. I'm not saying that promoting this award is a bad thing, it's just not what Michigan does. What do you think Robert Griffin III winning the Heisman will do for a program like Baylor?

The pressure today on universities and coaches to succeed is incredible. Each year coaches are being hired with bonus incentives to **_WIN_** a National Championship. Universities also see the Heisman Trophy as a tremendous opportunity to build their program by attracting the best recruits in America. When Joey Harrington, the Oregon quarterback at the time entered his senior season they promoted him. In 2001 some University of Oregon boosters put up a Joey Harrington billboard in New York City, for a rumored $250,000. That was a mere 2913 miles from campus. They were attempting to boost his national recognition to gain Heisman votes. Harrington finished 4th that year, 406 votes behind the winner, Eric Crouch, the quarterback from Nebraska.

Oregon is not the only university that promotes the Heisman Trophy at that level. I can tell you that other schools have spent and done more. The memories and stories of these discussions, campaigns, and the heated debates surrounding the award are a unique part of College Football's history. More recently, there has been controversy and doubt surrounding candidates and winners. Reggie Bush even returned his award when violations were discovered years after he left USC. During Cam Newton's storied season in 2010, there were investigations into his recruiting. Time will tell where that story ends.

So with so much focus on this individual award, let me get back to this story, and the University of Michigan. Bo Schembechler took over as Michigan's coach in 1969. At the time this proud program had seen its' ups and downs. Michigan had won National Titles, Tom Harmon had already been awarded the Heisman Trophy in 1940, but things weren't the same at Michigan. The Big House wasn't full, and Michigan was in need of a change. Schembechler was hired and the legacies he set still stand to this day. Three of the last four coaches at Michigan have come from Bo's

coaching lineage. One thing that was very clear to Bo and those who have followed him was that Michigan isn't placing the Heisman above any team goals. It was pretty clear how Bo felt about individual honors. In 1983, Schembechler had this to say, his legendary speech, about the **TEAM:**

"We want the Big Ten championship, and we're going to win it as a team. They can throw out all those great backs and great quarterbacks and great defensive players through the country and in this conference, but there's going to be one team that plays solely as a team. No man is more important than the team, no coach is more important than the team. The team, the team, the team!
"If we think that way? All of us? Everything you do, take into consideration what effect does it have on my team? Because you can go into professional football, you can go anywhere you want to play after you leave here. You will never play for a team again. You'll play for a contract, you'll play for this, you'll play for that. You'll play for everything except the team. Think what a great thing it is to be part of

something that is the team! "We're going to win it.
We're going to win the championship again because
we're going to play as a team. Better than anybody
else in this conference, we're going to play together
as a team. We're going to believe in each other, were
not going to criticize each other, we're not going to
talk about each other. We're going to encourage
each other! "When we play as a team, when the old
season is over, you and I know it's going to be
Michigan again. MICHIGAN."

Nowhere in that speech did he speak about an All-American

honor, an All-Big Ten Team, or the Heisman Memorial

Trophy. That's not what it's about at Michigan. It has

always been about playing hard, winning the Big Ten,

beating ohio state, and winning a bowl game or National

Championship. I understand that as a true fan and so do

most players who put on the Maize and Blue. This program

and its' successes have come from the mindset, players, and

coaches that understood those goals long before and after

Bo's remarks in 1983. For Bo, players came to Michigan to

play for Michigan. Many moved on to the NFL. Some

finished high in the Heisman voting, but it wasn't the focus

of those teams. Was Bo proud of them? Yes. Would he let

people know they were the best at their position? Certainly.

But the recognition came to hardworking players, with

natural ability, playing within the confines of the team.

When he had great players, he talked about how great they

were. He loved his players and hoped for their success at

Michigan. First however, he wanted them to play for Michigan and each other. College Football has changed a lot since 1983.

Players come to Michigan and other universities for various reasons. Some want the quality education. Some want to wear the winged helmet and play in the Big House. Others come because they know they will be on TV every week, and they see the number of Michigan players filling out NFL rosters. Some probably even want to win the Heisman, but I don't think they told Bo or any other Michigan coach that. When they arrive in Ann Arbor, they find themselves a member of a team. The team with the most wins in the History of College Football. The team with three goals each year. Despite three winners in the last seventy-one years and others who came close, the Heisman has never been the goal.

With that being said however, 21 total Michigan players have placed in the Top Ten Voting for the Award with a few placing in multiple seasons bringing the total to 26. 35 total schools in the 120 FBCS schools have had a player win the Heisman Memorial Trophy. Notre Dame and ohio state each have had 7 winners, USC 6, and Oklahoma 5. Michigan ranks 5th with their 3 winners along with Army, Auburn, Florida, and Nebraska. The award is mostly associated with the best programs in the sport.

This story is about the players throughout Michigan's history that have elevated themselves into the Heisman Trophy discussion while leading their teams to perform at a higher level. Several have worked within the team to garner national recognition, and three have won the coveted award. When Michigan football teams took the field in 1940, 1991, and 1997, they didn't take the field to bring the Heisman to Ann Arbor. The players who did were exceptional talents, playing on teams with the goal of winning a championship. Each was unique, but there are some common threads that will forever unite these players. As you learn more about Michigan's storied history with the Heisman, keep 3 things in mind.

THESE GUYS WEREN'T RUDY, THESE GUYS WEREN'T WALK ONS.

Each was a high school superstar, with the chance to go to several programs. Secondly,

THEY CAME FROM RIVAL STATES

and Michigan was able to lure them out of Big Ten rival areas in the Midwest. These three men were from enemy territory. The third is that each:

SEALED THE DEAL AGAINST THE BUCKEYES IN THE SEASON FINALE

As we explore each and every player at Michigan that challenged for the Heisman Trophy, defined by finishing the annual voting in the Top Ten, we will review the *"THREE*

MICHIGAN HEISMAN CRITERIA." Although the analysis is less than scientific, it relates the common threads that these Michigan players shared. They also started their Heisman seasons with big games early and provided highlights and performances that are legendary to this day. Each also had a unique appearance characteristic from tear away jerseys and ankle tape to high white socks. Some of the players who came close had all of the criteria, some had one, some two, some none. Those who came close are also Michigan legends. They helped build this great program, and define the widely known, but loosely defined, **MICHIGAN MAN.**

What makes a **MICHIGAN MAN?** We as fans will never completely know. I don't believe that Heisman votes make a **MICHIGAN MAN.** I think for each player I cover in this story, there are hundreds more that have earned the title despite never receiving a Heisman vote. Being one of these men, in my humble opinion as an outsider, is something that they are long after their playing days, but also that the character they display was partially developed in the Big House. Lloyd Carr, the retired Michigan Coach who led the Wolverines to the 1997 National Championship once said that these men are those who *"deeply love the University of Michigan."* There are thousands of these men and this story is not meant to slight any of them. Gerald Ford left Michigan and became the President of the United States.

He isn't part of this story. Growing up, Michigan great Jamie Morris visited our home, and spent time with the Gallagher Five. We met Jumbo Elliot, Phil Webb, and others. It breaks my heart not to fully include these players in this collection. There were linebackers, tackles, guards, fullbacks,

safeties, punters, and kickers at Michigan that were All-Big Ten and All-Americans. They will never be forgotten and played at a high level on each of these teams. However, not all of them are in this story. Many greats will be left out, but understand *I KNOW*. This story is about those who played for the Wolverines and finished in the Top Ten of the Heisman Balloting from 1940 to today. This story will cover each one, and outline some information that will give even the biggest Michigan Fan a new appreciation of some of the legends that have helped build the program that is today. On and off the field, these are stories that have never been collected together. As you will see however, they should have been long ago. It is a story 71 years in the making that re-defines the **MICHIGAN MAN** from World War II heroes to today's big hearted philanthropists. Each player has his own amazing story. In the end, only three, *# 98, # 21, and # 2,* had or have a Heisman Trophy in the den, so let's get started with first.

98

TOM HARMON
SETTING THE STANDARD

Michigan's first Heisman came to Ann Arbor in 1940. The winner was Tom Harmon, the original Michigan Superstar. On and off the field, Harmon was bigger than life. Many believe he was Michigan's all-time greatest player, even today. Harmon grew up in Rensselaer, Indiana. During his early years, his family moved to Gary, Indiana where grew up near the steel mills. He had 4 brothers and 2 sisters and I can certainly relate to that. I am one of five, and big families make you tough. Harmon's journey began in that Midwestern blue collar town, a far cry from the many journeys he took during his life.

Before arriving at Michigan, he had the first characteristic, he was an outstanding athlete. He worked hard and would not be discouraged. He made an immediate impact when he played high school football. The facts of the story may never be completely confirmed, but Harmon's football story began as a freshman. He chewed gum constantly and his coach had finally had enough. He was told to take off his jersey, and was then directed to return kickoffs against the varsity team. He was about to learn his lesson right? They kicked the ball to Harmon and instead of being punished, he scored. They kicked the ball, he scored. The day that began in the dog house, was the opportunity he needed to showcase his extreme talent. Harmon was told to retrieve his jersey. Confident, he returned with one of the varsity player's jerseys, rumored to be the team star's.

Naturally, Harmon was told to take it off. Denied again, but unfazed Harmon donned #98, and wore it for the rest of his career. That high school was called Horace Mann, and Harmon graduated in 1937. He earned varsity letters in several sports, and 14 in total. He was twice an All-State quarterback. His idol at the time was Jay Berwanger, the first winner of the Heisman Memorial Trophy.

He was recruited by several schools, but was lured to Michigan. He had two brothers playing College Football, one of which played at Purdue University in Indiana. Most thought he would follow his brother to Purdue. Michigan had gone through a terrible stretch from 1934 to 1936 and the Coach at the time, Harry Kipke, was under **"RODRIGUEZ- LIKE"** scrutiny. Michigan went 6-18 during that span, yet for Harmon, the choice was the Wolverines. It was a different game back then, but it was even rumored that Harmon received financial help from boosters to make up his mind. In 1937, the Wolverines went 4-4. It was an improvement but not enough to save Kipke's job. Harmon didn't contribute on the varsity as a freshman (typical at the time) while weathering the storm surrounding his recruitment.

Fritz Crisler arrived in Ann Arbor and put Harmon to work in 1938. Harmon made his debut on the varsity squad at Michigan. He played in all 8 games and led the team in rushing with 398 yards rushing and 3 touchdowns.

He averaged 5.17 yards per carry, and also passed for 310 yards and 3 touchdowns. It was a different game in Harmon's era, and although he was a right halfback, he was also the Wolverine's leading passer. The TEAM went 6-1, and tied for second place in the Big Ten. Michigan was making the turn, and Harmon was establishing himself as a very good College Football player. The season ended with an 18-0 victory over ohio state. Harmon started setting the standard for Michigan players on that day, running for a touchdown, throwing another, and intercepting a pass. Bring it home against the buckeyes...

In 1939, Harmon garnered national recognition and Michigan continued its' team success. Michigan finished 4th in a competitive Big Ten Conference, with a 6-2 overall record. Harmon rushed for 884 yards and 13 touchdowns, averaging 6.8 yards per carry. Again, Harmon led the team in passing with 538 yards and 6 touchdowns. In 1939, he even started kicking PATs, connecting on 15 of 22. Harmon was becoming a star. Michigan played Iowa that season, and Harmon went head to head with Nile Kinnick, the 1939 Heisman winner. Harmon was up to the challenge. Iowa came to Michigan Stadium, and Harmon outscored the Hawkeyes and their Heisman Trophy candidate 27-7. Michigan lost to Illinois and Minnesota and faced ohio state in the season finale. Once again Harmon and the Wolverines won 21-14 on a late fake kick. The Wolverines were prepped for a big year in 1940, and the guy from Gary, Indiana was being talked about across the nation.

1939 HEISMAN VOTING RESULTS:

PLACE	NAME	SCHOOL	CLASS	POSTION	POINTS
1	NILE KINNICK	IOWA	SR.	HB	651
2	TOM HARMON*	MICHIGAN	JR.	HB	405
3	PAUL CHRISTMAN	MISSOURI	JR.	QB	391
4	GEORGE CAFEGO	TENNESSEE	SR.	TB	296

And then in 1940, it happened. Harmon and Michigan opened the 1940 season at the University of California. It was a Hollywood debut for Harmon. Michigan won the game 41-0, and Harmon ran wild. He took the opening kickoff for a touchdown and never looked back. Michigan went 7-1 in 1940, falling only to the Big Ten Champion, Minnesota. On November 9th, 1940, Michigan lost at Minnesota 7-6. The game had some controversy, but Minnesota was a great team. Harmon and the Wolverines moved on. They won the rest of their games and on November 23rd, with "THAT" game against the buckeyes, Harmon brought home the Heisman Memorial Trophy.

The game was in Columbus, and Harmon put on a show. He rushed for 139 yards and 2 touchdowns. He

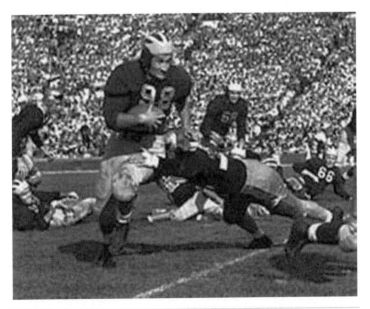

completed 11 of 12 passes, for 151 yards, and 2 more touchdowns. He intercepted 3 passes, returning one for another score. He also kicked four extra points. On that day in enemy territory, Harmon set the standard for future Michigan players. The ohio state crowd even gave Harmon a standing ovation, and I assure you that will never happen again. Sorry Denard Robinson, even with a big win in 2012, I think that was it.

1940 HEISMAN VOTING RESULTS

PLACE	NAME	SCHOOL	CLASS	POSITION	POINTS
1	TOM HARMON*	MICHIGAN	Sr.	HB	1,303
2	JOHN KIMBROUGH	TEXAS A&M	SR.	RB	841
3	GEORGE FRANCK	MINNESOTA	SR.	HB	102
4	FRANKIE ALBERT	STANFORD	JR.	QB	90
5	PAUL CHRISTMAN	MISSOURI	SR.	QB	66

Harmon started another tradition for Michigan Heisman winners while running wild in the Big Ten. After watching the unstoppable Harmon being tackled by his jersey, which was the only thing opponents could catch time after time, Michigan would put him in a tear away one. As you'll see going forward, all Michigan's winners had a uniform trait. Mr. Harmon was the trend-setter in every way.

TOM HARMON

#98

ATTRIBUTES:

1. POWERFUL RUNNING STYLE
2. SPEED
3. THE TEAR AWAY JERSEY
4. BORN LEADER WHO WANTED TO WIN

THE STATISTICS

RUSHING

YEAR	ATTEMPTS	YARDS	AVERAGE	TOUCHDOWNS
1938	77	398	5.17	3
1939	130	884	6.8	13
1940	191	852	4.46	14
CAREER	398	2134	5.36	30

PASSING

YEAR	ATTEMPTS	COMP	YARDS	TOUCHDOWNS
1938	45	21	310	3
1939	94	37	538	6
1940	94	43	506	7
CAREER	233	101	1354	16

KICK RETURNS

YEAR	RETURNS	YARDS	AVERAGE	TOUCHDOWNS
1938	0	0	0	0
1939	4	92	23	0
1940	6	204	34	1
CAREER	10	296	29.6	1

PUNT RETURNS

YEAR	RETURNS	YARDS	AVERAGE	TOUCDOWNS
1938	2	11	5.5	0
1939	1	10	10	0
1940	19	234	12.3	0
CAREER	22	255	12.5	0

PASS INTERCEPTIONS

YEAR	INTERCEPTIONS	YARDS	AVERAGE	TOUCHDOWNS
1938	1	16	16	0
1939	3	98	32.6	1
1940	4	30	7.5	1
CAREER	8	144	18	2

KICKING

YEAR	PUNTS	YARDS	PATs	FIELD GOALS
1938	0	0	0/1	0
1939	2	110	15/22	1
1940	42	1557	18/28	1
CAREER	44	1667	33/51	2

ALL CONFERENCE TEAMMATES:

Forest Evashevski, Edward Frutig, Ralph Fritz

ALL AMERICAN TEAMMATES:

Edward Frutig

INDIVIDUAL AWARDS:

The Heisman Memorial Trophy, The Walter Camp Award, The Maxwell Award, AP Offensive Player of the Year, The Dunlop Pro-Am Athlete of the Year

OTHER NOTABLES:

Michigan's original superstar, war hero, and famed broadcaster

THE MOMENT:

Closed out his career with the greatest game ever by a Michigan player, passing for two touchdowns, running for two touchdowns, and intercepting 3 passes. He even kicked the extra points and received a standing ovation from the hostile crowd in Columbus.

His life after Michigan was even more amazing. Instead of moving on to NFL stardom, Harmon headed out to Hollywood, and filmed his first movie, <u>Harmon of Michigan</u>, a story based loosely on his playing days. The movie wasn't very successful, but with the money he did earn Harmon built his parents a house. He appeared in eighteen movies total, but never could dreamed of what would come from his time in Hollywood. Harmon met his wife, a Hollywood starlet named Elyse Knox. Harmon was

in love, but with the world at war, he enlisted in United States Army Air Corps. He flew P-38 and B-25 bombers and fought in World War II. He was twice reported missing. He was first reported missing in South America, and survived four days in the swamplands and jungles of French Guiana. He was eventually rescued by friendly locals. His aircraft went down again in China and of the eight Army Air Corps personnel on that aircraft, only Harmon made it out alive and parachuted into enemy territory near the Yangtze River. He reportedly acted dead, and was eventually smuggled to safety by Chinese natives. The media had already reported him missing and that it was unlikely that he had survived. Harmon did survive, returned home, and earned the Silver Star. **MICHIGAN MAN!**

As I researched for this book, I wondered how much I knew about Tom Harmon. I knew that he was perhaps the greatest player in Michigan history. I even knew that he served in the Army before attempting an NFL career, but his story became more and more amazing with each piece of information that I learned.

I know a little about the Military. I come from a line of Army Officers. My father is a retired Army Colonel. My three brothers and I were, or are, Officers in the United States Army. We have deployed for this great country, and I spent a year in a place called Iraq with the 82nd Airborne. I got shot at, got scared, felt the adrenaline, and came home safe. I was even awarded a Bronze Star. Never however, did I experience anything like Harmon's story. The Silver Star is one of the highest military decorations awarded. The Silver Star is awarded for gallantry in action against an enemy of the United States not justifying the Distinguished Service Cross, the Navy Cross, the Air Force Cross, or the Medal of Honor. It is awarded to service members who display extraordinary heroism. Harmon was not just a Michigan hero; he was an American hero and patriot.

In 1944 after his service, Harmon married Elyse Knox. His best friend and teammate at Michigan, quarterback Forest Evashevski was his best man. Knox's dress was partially made from the very silk of the parachute that saved his life. As a former paratrooper, all I can say is AMAZING. My grandmother, 87 years old, further informed me that there was more to the story. It turns out most of silk in the United States was being utilized for the military, and that Elyse was very lucky to have some in her dress. Thanks Grandma, I love you. She is the same lady who bought me my very first pair of screw in football cleats and whose backyard has as many memories as the East sideline in the Big House.

After the Military, he and Elyse settled in Los Angeles, CA where she continued her acting career. That Harmon had style. I proposed to my wife backstage in front of our favorite country music star and surprised him as much as her. The more I learned about Harmon, the more I liked his style. After his wedding Tom made his long awaited NFL debut, playing for the Los Angeles Rams. Harmon felt the physical effects of the War. He never displayed the power or explosiveness that he displayed at Michigan. During his two years with the Rams, Harmon rushed for 542 yards and accumulated 9 total touchdowns. After retirement from the NFL, Harmon entered a career in broadcasting, full time.

He had opportunities and the interest before, but didn't concentrate on it full time. Once he did, Harmon had a long and successful career in broadcasting. If you look at all of the successful athletes and coaches who have made the transition to the broadcast booth, this Michigan hero was the trend setter. Harmon paved the way for former Michigan heroes to follow to include Brian Griese and Desmond Howard. He worked for CBS and ABC, while covering various sports. He and Elyse had 3 children; Mark, Kelly, and Kristin. Mark Harmon, an established actor, played quarterback at UCLA, and Tom had the privilege of covering some of his son's games, starting another Michigan tradition that would be followed by Bob and Brian Griese. Tom Harmon died in 1990, at the age of 70, of a heart attack. His amazing life and experiences set the standard for any **MICHIGAN MAN** that would follow.

1941-1968
THOSE WHO CAME CLOSE

1941, BOB WESTFALL # 86

It didn't take long for Michigan to have another candidate. He actually shared the backfield with Harmon as a sophomore and junior. Bob Westfall (#86) kept things rolling after Harmon left. He played for Michigan from 1939 to 1941. During 1940 there were even games when Westfall was the headliner, and their rushing statistics will surprise many Michigan fans. Fans like me who knew more about Harmon. In 1940 as Harmon raced to the Heisman Trophy, there was Westfall, the fullback, leading the way. Harmon ran for 852 yards and 14 touchdowns. What is less known is that in 1940, Bob Westfall ran for 808 yards and a less glamorous 3 touchdowns. In a game against Illinois that season, Westfall ran for 152 yards during a 28-0 victory. The media outlined that Westfall stole the show that day. Against Northwestern, during a 20-13 victory, Westfall scored two touchdowns and won the game late with a tackle that held Northwestern out of the end zone. In 1941, Westfall kept the Wolverines rolling. His physical running style and ability to keep his balance performing the spin move were tough to stop. His spin move would have made any Madden player proud. He led the Wolverines with 688 yards rushing as the feature back, and 7 more touchdowns. In 1941, Westfall finished 8th in the Heisman balloting, with running back Bruce Smith of Minnesota the winner. In 1941, Michigan went 6-1-1 and finished fifth in the nation. He was a first team All-American at fullback.

1941 HEISMAN VOTING RESULTS

PLACE	NAME	SCHOOL	CLASS	POSITION	POINTS
1	BRUCE SMITH	MINNESOTA	SR.	HB	554
2	ANGELO BERTILLI	NOTRE DAME	SO.	QB	345
3	FRANKIE ALBERT	STANFORD	SR.	QB	336
4	FRANK SINKWICH	GEORGIA	JR.	HB	249
5	BILL DUDLEY	VIRGINIA	SR.	HB	237
6	ENDICOTT PEABODY	HARVARD	SR.	G	153
7	EDGAR JONES	PITT	SR.	RB	151
8	BOB WESTFALL*	MICHIGAN	SR.	FB	147
9	STEVE LACH	DUKE	SR.	HB	126
10	JACK CRAIN	TEXAS	SR.	RB	102

Westfall was another Michigan great, but there were several factors that didn't meet the *"THREE MICHIGAN*

HEISMAN CRITERIA." First, Westfall wasn't from enemy territory, not at all. Westfall was from Ann Arbor, Michigan. For those who know Ann Arbor, he went to Tappan Junior High and Ann Arbor High School like my brothers. He wasn't quite the mega recruit that Harmon was. In his final game against the buckeyes, the Wolverines tied 20-20. Westfall did have a big day with 162 yards and he will always be a Michigan great, but he was not a Heisman Trophy winner. He certainly further defined the **MICHIGAN MAN** and the great program that Michigan is today.

After football, Westfall too served his country. He also enlisted in the Army Air Corps. Ultimately Westfall would suffer from air sickness and his time flying was short lived. Health issues ultimately resulted in his discharge from the Army Air Corps. In 1944, Westfall returned to Michigan to complete his degree while working in a manufacturing plant. Later in 1944, despite questions about him playing again for Michigan Westfall signed with the Detroit Lions. After retiring from the NFL in 1947, he would enter the Steel Industry in Michigan and eventually became the President of The Adrian Steel Company. He would also coach a semi-pro team in Adrian. Bob Westfall died in 1980 at the age of 61. As I look on the back of my work truck each day, I stare at a tool box made by Adrian Steel. Just a small reminder of the work of a **MICHIGAN MAN.**

1943, WILLIAM EDWARD "BULLET" DALEY # 45

Bill Daley played for the Wolverines in 1943. Daley's Michigan career consisted of six games at fullback. In those six games he rushed for 817 yards. He was named an All-American, and finished 6th in the Heisman Trophy balloting. Angelo Bertelli, the Notre Dame quarterback was the winner. Daley's journey to Michigan was one of the most unique. From 1940-1941, while Westfall and Harmon battled Minnesota for the Big Ten title and the Heisman Trophy, Daley was a Gopher. In 1943 Daley enlisted in the Navy. His Navy journey led him to the University of Michigan. He is the only player in the history of the Michigan and Minnesota Rivalry to win the "Little Brown Jug" on both sides of the rivalry. At the time, with the heat of the rivalry between Michigan and Minnesota, it is comparable to the Justin Boren saga of today (except Boren would be a Heisman candidate). Boren was a Michigan lineman who transferred to ohio state. Daley went 4-0 in the rivalry, playing on both sides, and knew ALL about the "Little Brown Jug."

1943 HEISMAN VOTING RESULTS

PLACE	NAME	SCHOOL	CLASS	POSITION	POINTS
1	ANGELO BERTELLI	NOTRE DAME	SR.	QB	648
2	BOB ODELL	PENNSYLVANIA	SR.	B	177
3	OTTO GRAHAM	NORTHWESTERN	SR.	QB	140
4	CREIGHTON MILLER	NOTRE DAME	SR.	HB	134
5	EDDIE PROKOP	GEORGIA TECH	SR.	RB	85
6	HAL HAMBURG	NAVY	JR.	HB	73
7	BILL DALEY*	MICHIGAN	SR.	FB	71
8	TONY BUTKOVICH	PURDUE	SO.	FB	65
9	JIM WHITE	NOTRE DAME	SR.	T	52

Daley led Michigan to an 8-1 record, with a lone loss to Notre Dame and Heisman winner Angelo Bertelli. Head to head, Michigan defeated Northwestern (led by Otto Graham) another Heisman candidate. As far as the formula goes, I will admit that Daley is one of my anomalies. He was clearly from enemy territory and good enough to play for national powerhouse Minnesota before playing for the Wolverines. In his final game, in 1943, Michigan blasted the buckeyes, 45-7. Although Daley did not win the Heisman Trophy, he had the *"THREE MICHIGAN HEISMAN CRITERIA,"* and elevated Michigan during the 1943 season. Daley was another superstar, veteran, and tradition builder for the Wolverines.

After leaving Michigan, he played professional football for the Brooklyn Dodgers, the Miami Seahawks, Chicago Rockets, and New York Yankees in the All

American Football Conference. He eventually returned to the University of Minnesota to complete his degree. His new career would lead him into the broadcast booth, like Harmon, where he spent 10 years covering the Golden Gophers and the Minnesota Vikings. In the 1970's Daley became an art dealer and eventually opened his own gallery. Another **MICHIGAN MAN** who was so much more than a football player.

1947, ROBERT "BOB" CHAPPUIS # 49

In 1947, Michigan came close again. Robert Richard "Bob" Chappuis played for the Wolverines in 1942, 1946, and 1947. He played both halfback and quarterback. Along with the others, the nation was at war, and his career was interrupted by his service in the Air Force during World War II. Like Harmon, his time serving this great country was exciting if you can call it that. He flew 21 combat missions as a radio operator and an aerial gunner on B-25 Bombers. His aircraft was shot down in February,

1945, and amazingly, despite landing in Northern Italy, Chappuis survived. He spent 3 months with his co-survivors, living with Italians, and waiting out the conclusion of the war. I have been a Michigan fan since the late 1980's, when my memories began. Like Harmon however, as an Army Officer and a paratrooper, these stories I have found during my research are amazing. My thoughts and understanding of the **MICHIGAN MAN** grew and changed with Bob Chappuis.

He returned to Michigan in 1947 after his service and led the "Mad Magicians" to an undefeated season, climaxing with a 49-0 win over USC in the Rose Bowl. #49 finished the season with 1,164 yards passing and was one of the sports first passing specialists.

1949 ROSE BOWL

Scoring		MICH		USC
First Quarter				
M	Weisenburger, 1-yard run (Brieske kick)	21	First Downs	10
Second Quarter		219	Net Yards Rushing	91
M	Weisenburger, 1-yard run (Brieske kick)	272	Net Yards Passing	42
M	Bump Elliott, 11-yard pass from Chappuis (Brieske kick)	72	Total Plays	55
		491	Total Yards	133
Third Quarter		27/17/1	PA/PC/Int	11/6/1
M	Yerges, 18-yard pass from Chappuis (Brieske kick)	4/38.3	Punts/Avg.	8/43.8
		60	Return Yards	16
Fourth Quarter		2/1	Fumbles/Lost	4/2
M	Weisenburger, 1-yard run (Brieske kick)	4/40	Penalties/Yards	1/10
M	Derricotte, 45-yard pass from Fonde (Brieske kick)	Rushing-- (M): Chappuis 13-91; Weisenburger 20-91; Ford 2-21; Derricotte 3-8; Peterson 1-4; Elliott 5-4; (SC): Garlin 5-25; Betz 4-16.		
M	Rifenburg, 29-yard pass from Yerges (Brieske kick)	Passing-- (M): Chappuis 14-24-188; Fonde 1-1-45; Yerges 1-1-29; Derricotte 1-1-10; (SC): Powers 4-5-22; Robertson 1-1-22.		

MICHIGAN 49 USC 0

The Wolverines finished the regular season with a 21-0 win over ohio state. In his last game in Michigan Stadium that day, he accounted for 307 total yards. That record would stand for 20 years. For comparison, in the 2011 contest, Denard Robinson compiled 337 yards. That's right, Michigan had a guy doing "Shoelace" stuff in 1949, after Harmon left. The Wolverines finished 9-0, along with Notre Dame. During conference play Michigan outscored opponents 345-53. They finished 2nd in the rankings. In an unprecedented post bowl vote, Michigan garnered #1 after their performance against USC. The "Mad Magicians", led by #49, were the last team that the legendary Fritz Crisler would coach. Chappuis came closer than any other Michigan player to winning the Heisman Trophy who was not the winner. During this amazing season, he finished second, with John Lujack from Notre Dame winning the award.

1947 HEISMAN TROPHY VOTING RESULTS

PLACE	NAME	SCHOOL	CLASS	POSITION	POINTS
1	JOHN LUJACK	NOTRE DAME	SR.	QB	742
2	BOB CHAPPUIS*	MICHIGAN	SR.	HB	555
3	DOAK WALKER	SMU	SO.	HB	196
4	CHARLEY CONERLY	MISSISSIPPI	SR.	QB	186
5	HARRY GILMER	ALABAMA	SR.	HB	115
6	BOBBY LANE	TEXAS	SR.	QB	75
7	CHUCK BEDNARIK	PENNSYLVANIA	JR.	C	65
8	BILL SWIACKI	COLUMBIA	SR.	E	61

Again, Bob Chappuis completely challenges my *"THREE MICHIGAN HEISMAN CRITERIA,"* but would you expect anything else from these guys? Another American Hero, like our Grandfathers and Harmon, who fought the forces of evil so I can sit in the backyard and write this book today. The men of this era were the original definition of a **MICHIGAN MAN,** and heroes. Chappuis set Michigan total offense and passer rating records that stood into the Schembechler era. He was a great player, from Ohio, and certainly brought it home against the buckeyes. The annual award for the Nation's Top Running Back is named for the guy who finished behind him, Doak Walker.

Chappuis moved from Michigan to a career in the All American Football Conference, where he played for the Brooklyn Dodgers and Chicago Hornets. He would retire from football when the league folded in 1950. From there, Bob entered the business world, and held various positions in the Fort Wayne, Indiana area. In 1988, #49 was elected to the College Football Hall of Fame.

34 | 9 8 - 2 1 - 2

1955-1956, RON KRAMER # 87

Ron Kramer was an "END" playing both ways at the University of Michigan from 1954 to 1956. In 1955, Kramer finished 8th in the Heisman voting, while Howard Cassady, the halfback from ohio state was the winner. In a game against Missouri that year Kramer caught 7 passes for 109 yards and 3 touchdowns.

1956 HEISMAN VOTING RESULTS

PLACE	NAME	SCHOOL	CLASS	POSITION	1	2	3	TOTAL
1	PAUL HORNUNG	NOTRE DAME	SR.	QB	197	162	151	1066
2	JOHN MAJORS	TENNESSEE	SR.	RB	172	171	136	994
3	TOM MCDONALD	OKLAHOMA	SR.	HB	205	122	114	973
4	JERRY TUBBS	OKLAHOMA	SR.	C-LB	121	137	87	724
5	JIM BROWN	SYRACUSE	SR.	HB	118	68	71	561
6	RON KRAMER*	MICHIGAN	SR.	E	70	104	100	518
7	JOHN BRODIE	STANFORD	SR.	QB	39	52	60	281
8	JIM PARKER	OHIO STATE	SR.	G	34	51	44	248
9	KENNY PLOEN	IOWA	SR.	QB	36	10	22	150
10	JON ARNETT	USC	SR.	HB	20	25	18	128

In 1956, Kramer moved up to 6th in the voting, with Paul Horning of Notre Dame the winner. Kramer was a two-time All-America selection. Kramer is to this day, a Michigan great. He was a multi-sport star before it was trendy. He was a thousand point scorer for Michigan in basketball, and was also on the track team. Kramer is one of the greatest

Photo from the Michiganensian, 1956

athletes in Michigan history. There is no question about that. He was an All American in football in 1955 and 1956. He played offense and defense, and was known for his physical ability to block and tackle. His greatness on the football field for Michigan often wasn't measured on the stat sheet. Kramer was tough.

During his senior season the highly ranked Wolverines would be upset by Michigan State and would also lose to Minnesota. Although the losses were disappointing, you couldn't fault Kramer. He was all over the field, not only playing both ways, but even appeared as a punter, kicker and running back. This guy was an amazing athlete. His #87 jersey was retired following his senior season in 1956, only one of five retired at this great Michigan program. He finished his career with 53 catches for 880 yards and 8 touchdowns.

After Michigan, Kramer moved to the NFL where he had a successful career with the Green Bay Packers. He ended up playing with Hornung, and was a key blocker on the famed Green Bay packers "sweep" play. He was an All-Pro in 1962, and helped the Green Bay Packers win a Championship. He played ten total NFL seasons, seven with the Packers, and then three with the Detroit Lions. Between his time with the Packers and Lions, Kramer served five years in the United States Air Force. During his later years, Kramer always found time to be around the program. You could find him on Big Ten Network programs about Michigan Football, and even delivering apples to the players after practice. That tradition started during his playing days, and the **MICHIGAN MAN** continued it to the very end. Ron Kramer passed away September 11th, 2010. When it comes to the *"THREE MICHIGAN HEISMAN CRITERIA,"* here is how Kramer stacked up. He was a big time recruit, but he was also from Michigan. He did help Michigan beat the buckeyes 19-0 in 1956. Ron Kramer is an all-time Michigan great, and another definition of the kind of man that has made Michigan the program it is today.

1964, BOB TIMBERLAKE # 28

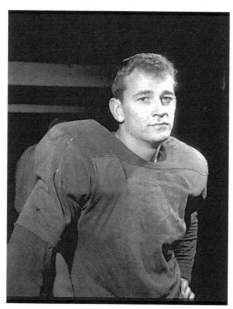

Bob Timberlake played for Michigan from 1962 to 1964. He was a highly recruited player and one of the first Michigan "NFL" built quarterbacks. He was 6'4" tall and around 210 pounds. His highlight season at Michigan came during his senior year. He led the Wolverines to the Big Ten Championship, and followed that up with a 34-7 victory over the Oregon State Beavers in the 1965 Rose Bowl Game. Michigan did drop one game that year, and that was against the Purdue Boilermakers, and a sophomore quarterback named Bob Griese. The 21-20 heartbreaker in Ann Arbor was Michigan's only loss of the year. Griese would go on to finish 2nd in the Heisman voting in 1966, but managed to lead Purdue over Michigan and end their National Title hopes. If you don't know, he also went on to be named to the NFL Hall of Fame, and sent a son to Michigan named

Brian, and was 3-0 against Michigan. More on that later, but back to Timberlake, and this story. In 1964, he also had a head to head matchup with Illinois and Dick Butkus. Butkus finished 3rd in the Heisman balloting in 1964.

Timberlake was the Big Ten's Most Valuable Player according to the Chicago Tribune. Over his career at Michigan, Timberlake passed for 1,507 yards, and was responsible for 19 total touchdowns. He also rushed for 315 yards. Timberlake was a true passing specialist, while that phase of the game continued to develop. Timberlake also kicked for the Wolverines on both punts and field goals. He connected on 36 extra points and six field goals, accounting for 121 points during his Wolverine career.

1964 HEISMAN VOTING RESULTS

PLACE	NAME	SCHOOL	CLASS	POSITION	POINTS
1	JOHN HUARTE	NOTRE DAME	SR.	QB	1,026
2	JERRY RHOME	TULSA	SR.	QB	952
3	DICK BUTKUS	ILLINOIS	SR.	C-LB	505
4	BOB TIMBERLAKE*	MICHIGAN	SR.	QB	361
5	JACK SNOW	NOTRE DAME	SR.	E	187
6	TUCKER FREDERICKSON	AUBURN	SR.	FB	184
7	CRAIG MORTON	CALIFORNIA	SR.	QB	181
8	STEVE DELONG	TENNESSEE	SR.	MG	176
9	COSMO IACAVAZZI	PRINCETON	SR.	RB	165
10	BRIAN PICCOLO	WAKE FOREST	SR.	RB	124

John Huarte, the senior quarterback from Notre Dame won the Heisman with 1026 total points, while Timberlake finished 4th with 361. He was from Ohio, came to Michigan, and beat ohio state at the horsehoe in his final game. His efforts on that Saturday, accounted for all 10 Michigan points in the 10-0 victory. He threw a touchdown pass to Jim Detwiler, and also converted a field goal. The win was the first for Michigan against their arch rival since 1959. It was even terrible back then and the streak was only 5 years. After their Rose Bowl victory, they finished #4 in the nation.

Although Timberlake had each of the *"THREE MICHIGAN HEISMAN CRITERIA"* he did not win the Heisman. Timberlake had a brief professional career, and was selected in both the NFL and AFL Drafts. In 1965, he played for the New York Giants, where he was utilized as a kicker. After the NFL, Timberlake became an ordained minister, and has been on the faculty of Marquette University where he teaches courses in affordable housing and community service. This **MICHIGAN MAN** is also known for his involvement with Habitat for Humanity. Timberlake is another Michigan great who challenged the criteria, but for the sake of this story, we again move on.

1968, RON JOHNSON # 40

Ron Johnson was a
halfback who played for
Michigan on the Varsity
squad from 1966-1968.
He was from Detroit,
Michigan and continued
Michigan's great running
back tradition during his
career. He was a high
school standout at
Detroit's Northwestern
High School, and arrived

at Michigan in 1965. Michigan was struggling some after Timberlake and company left, and Johnson provided some much needed hope. During his career, he broke nearly every Michigan rushing record. During his senior year, Johnson piled up 347 yards rushing in a game against Wisconsin. Not only was it a Michigan record, but at the time, a national record. His 1,021 yards rushing in 1968 were a record for the Big Ten Conference. He also had a game in which he scored FIVE touchdowns. The 1968 team captain set several Michigan records. The 347 yard game against Wisconsin, as well as a 270 yard outburst against Navy still stand as the 1st and 4th greatest single game rushing totals in Michigan history. His performance in 1968 garnered national attention. Johnson was a First Team All American, and finished sixth in the Heisman Trophy voting. The winner was O.J. Simpson from USC.

1968 HEISMAN VOTING RESULTS

PLACE	NAME	SCHOOL	CLASS	POSITION	1	2	3	TOTAL
1	O.J. SIMPSON	USC	SR.	TB	855	128	82	2853
2	LEROY KEYES	PURDUE	SR.	RB-CB	49	358	240	1103
3	TERRY HANRATTY	NOTRE DAME	SR.	QB	22	86	149	387
4	TED KWALICK	PENN STATE	SR.	TE	14	69	74	254
5	TED HENDRICKS	MIAMI (FLORIDA)	SR.	DE	7	52	49	174
6	RON JOHNSON*	MICHIGAN	SR.	RB	12	36	50	158
7	BOB DOUGLASS	KANSAS	SR.	QB	9	33	39	132
8	CHRIS GILBERT	TEXAS	SR.	RB	12	34	20	124
9	BRIAN DOWLING	YALE	SR.	QB	15	25	24	119

As far as the **"THREE MICHIGAN HEISMAN CRITERIA"** goes, for what it's worth, Johnson wasn't it. One of the greatest players in Michigan history was a big time recruit, but he was also from Detroit. Although his team beat the buckeyes as sophomore, in 1968 they fell 50-14 at ohio stadium. Johnson graduated from the Ross School of Business at Michigan in 1968. After his time as a Wolverine, Johnson continued to showcase his ability. He played in the NFL from 1969 to 1976. He had the first two 1000 yard seasons in New York Giants history during his pro career.

After his playing days, Johnson continued his success. Like others before him, Johnson further defined the **MICHIGAN MAN.** Johnson was inducted into the College Football Hall of Fame in 1992. In 2006, he was named the Chairman of the National Football Foundation and College Football Hall of Fame. Like the predecessors, Johnson was much more than a football player and continues to promote this great game.

1974-1986

BO'S HEISMAN CANDIDATES

1974, DENNIS FRANKLIN # 9

Dennis Franklin was a quarterback at the University of

Michigan from
1971-1974. He
was Bo's third
quarterback, and
one of the first that
he recruited.
Franklin grew up
in Ohio, where he
starred for
Massillon High
School. That team
outscored

opponents 412-29 during his final season. Massillon was
loaded with Division 1 talent, and Franklin's success led him
to Ann Arbor. From 1972 to 1974, Dennis Franklin was the
starter. He beat out Tom Slade, who started in 1971. In that
period, Michigan and rival ohio state tied for 3 consecutive Big
Ten Championships. The team's overall record was thirty

wins, two losses, and one tie. He was the second player since Tom Harmon to lead Michigan in total offense every year he played. One of his most memorable moments at Michigan came against ohio state as a junior at the Big House. Entering the game, ohio state was ranked #1. Michigan entered the game ranked # 4. Ohio state had outscored opponents 361-63, and Michigan had kept pace outscoring opponents 320-58. The hype around the matchup was similar to that of "THE GAME" in 2006. In a classic battle, the game ended in a 10-10 tie. During the game, Franklin broke his collarbone. With another tie in the Big Ten, the Big Ten Athletic Directors had to decide who would play in the Rose Bowl game. Due to Franklin's injury, they selected ohio state, out of concern that Franklin would not play. In 1974, as team captain, Franklin was All Big Ten, and an Honorable Mention All American. He finished sixth in the Heisman balloting.

1974 HEISMAN VOTING RESULTS

PLACE	NAME	SCHOOL	CLASS	POSITION	1	2	3	TOTAL
1	ARCHIE GRIFFIN	OHIO STATE	JR.	RB	483	198	75	1920
2	ANTHONY DAVID	USC	SR.	TB	120	148	163	819
3	JOE WASHINGTON	OKLAHOMA	JR.	HB	87	146	108	661
4	TOM CLEMENTS	NOTRE DAME	SR.	QB	26	49	68	244
5	DAVID HUMM	NEBRASKA	SR.	QB	23	46	49	210
6	DENNIS FRANKLIN*	MICHIGAN	SR.	QB	6	30	22	100
7	ROD SHOATE	OKLAHOMA	SR.	LB	12	16	29	97
8	GARY SHEIDE	BYU	Sr.	QB	12	19	16	90

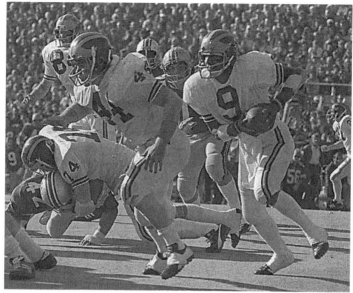

The winner in 1974 was Archie Griffin from ohio state.

In 1974, Franklin passed for 933 yards and 8 touchdowns.
He also ran for 290 yards and 5 more touchdowns. In a head
to head matchup with Archie Griffith, Dennis Franklin
passed for 96 yards and a score, but was also intercepted
twice. He was held to 11 yards rushing. Archie Griffin ran
for 111 yards on 25 carries, and won the Heisman Trophy.
Dennis Franklin was one of the greatest Michigan
quarterbacks of all time. His record as a starting quarterback
speaks for itself. Another consideration in Franklin's senior
season is that he shared the backfield with two great running
backs, Gordon Bell and Rob Lytle. When it comes to the
"THREE MICHIGAN HEISMAN CRITERIA" Dennis
Franklin was from enemy territory, Ohio. He was also a

sought after recruit. Against the buckeyes however, Franklin finished his career 0-2-1.

Franklin left Michigan and had a brief NFL career with the Detroit Lions. Many will remember Franklin as Michigan's first "black" quarterback, but Franklin had no interest in carrying that tag. He spoke about the topic years later and stated that it came up in just about every interview and that eventually it went away. A true **MICHIGAN MAN,** Franklin simply wanted to be known as the great Michigan quarterback and leader that he was. It is a fact that Franklin was Michigan's first African American quarterback. He paved the way in a different era for players like Michael Taylor, Demetrius Brown, Denard Robinson and Devin Gardner. The fact that he had to handle the questions, and how he handled it all, is just another reason why Dennis Franklin was a Michigan great. A quarterback whose teams won 90% of their games, and that is what he should be known for. After football, Franklin continued to lead. He rose to Vice President of a broadcasting company in New York City that produced many well know television shows. I believe Franklin now resides in California, working in Real Estate. Franklin like these other Michigan greats, proved to be much more than a football player.

1975, GORDON BELL # 5

It didn't take long after Franklin before Michigan had another stand out to compete with Archie Griffin. In 1973 and 1974, there was someone in the backfield with Franklin, Gordon Bell. Gordon Bell was from Troy, Ohio. He was a high school superstar, and got recruiting attention from several schools. Even in high school, Bell competed for honors with Archie Griffin. Gary Moeller, a Michigan Assistant Coach at the time, who would eventually be Bo Schembechler's successor, recruited Bell. Despite his accomplishments in high school, Bell was not your typical Big Ten back. He was around 5'9" tall and 175 pounds. Still, Moeller knew he had found a player.

Bo Schembechler called Bell, "the greatest cutback runner I've ever coached," in 1975. Famed Michigan radio broadcaster Bob Ufer called him, "Little Gordy Bell," during his time at Michigan. He also stated that Bell could "run

fifteen minutes in a phone booth and never touch the sides."
The diminutive Bell rushed for over 2,900 yards in his
Michigan career with 28 touchdowns. He first saw game
action in 1973 as a sophomore, but did not see game action
with Franklin and the others in the 10-10 tie with ohio state.
He amassed 464 yards in 1973, but did not score a
touchdown. In 1974, Bell broke into the lineup and rushed
for 1,048 yards, scoring 11 touchdowns. He had games of
134, 159, 142, 166, and 108 yards in Big Ten play. Bell
shared the backfield and carries with a talented sophomore
named Rob Lytle. In a win against Minnesota in 1974, the
two combined to rush for 292 yards.

More would follow in 1975, Bell's senior season.
Gordon Bell rushed for a total of 1,390 yards. He also added
314 yards on kick returns, and 84 yards receiving. He had
14 total touchdowns, 13 rushing. Even with those numbers
however, all the Heisman talk was about Griffin, the 1974
Heisman Trophy winner from "that school" to the south.

In 1975, Griffin averaged 123.7 yards per game in
the Big Ten. Bell led the Big Ten in rushing yards per game
at 134.1. To open the season, Michigan was ranked #3 in the
country. They faced Wisconsin in their first game. In the
23-6 Michigan victory, Gordon Bell carried the ball 28
times, and gained 210 yards. Even more amazing was that
Bell wasn't 100%. He had a pulled muscle in his leg. He
outlined that as a senior, it was his duty to play hurt,

MICHIGAN MAN. Following Wisconsin, the Wolverines tied games against Stanford and Baylor. Following those two games, Michigan won seven consecutive games with Bell as the feature back.

In the season finale against the buckeyes, the Wolverines fell 21-14. In the game, Gordon Bell outrushed the soon to be repeat Heisman Trophy winner 124 yards to 46 yards. Bell even threw a touchdown pass in the game. Bell spoke publicly about his comparisons and lack of publicity versus what Griffin received throughout their careers. He said that he did not feel Archie was the best running back in the Big Ten, much less the nation. And we wonder why Michigan and ohio state are the greatest rivalry in sports? Another factor in Gordon Bell's competition with Griffin and the Heisman was that he shared the backfield and carries with Rob Lytle. Bo Schembechler and the Wolverines had a talented team, and I have already outlined that individual awards were not Schembechler's or Michigan's goal in any season. In 1975, the Wolverines were loaded with talent. Freshman Rich Leach was the quarterback. In addition to Bell's 1,390 yards rushing, Rob Lytle rushed for 1,043 yards and 10 touchdowns. Although the lack of attention Bell seemed to receive compared to Griffin was outlined publicly, he also shared time at Michigan with another great back.

1975 HEISMAN TROPHY VOTING RESULTS

PLACE	NAME	SCHOOL	CLASS	POSITION	1	2	3	TOTAL
1	ARCHIE GRIFFIN	OHIO STATE	SR.	RB	454	167	104	1800
2	CHUCK MUNCIE	CALIFORNIA	SR.	TB	145	104	87	730
3	RICKY BELL	USC	JR.	TB	70	169	160	708
4	TONY DORSETT	PITTSBURGH	JR.	RB	66	149	120	616
5	JOE WASHINGTON	OKLAHOMA	SR.	HB	29	47	69	250
6	JIMMY DUBOSE	FLORIDA	SR.	RB	19	13	29	112
7	JOHN SCIARRA	UCLA	SR.	QB	12	15	20	86
8	GORDON BELL*	MICHIGAN	SR.	TB	2	27	24	84
9	LEROY SELMON	OKLAHOMA	SR.	DT	7	22	14	79
10	GENE SWICK	TOLEDO	SR.	QB	5	19	20	73

After his playing days at Michigan, Bell was selected in the fourth round of the NFL draft by the New York Giants. Bell had a short NFL career playing for the Giants and Cardinals, but never really broke through. He retired from football and managed a restaurant and more recently sells radio advertising in the Midwest. As far as the *"THREE MICHIGAN HEISMAN CRITERIA"* go, Bell was from Ohio. He was big time recruit who Gary Moeller lured to Michigan, but despite great games against the buckeyes, Gordon Bell finished 0-2-1. Gordon Bell was an outstanding running back for the University of Michigan, but for the sake of this story we move on to another guy in those great backfields.

1976, ROB LYTLE # 41

Rob Lytle was a running back for the Michigan Wolverines from 1973 to 1976. He was from Fremont, Ohio, and debated whether to attend Michigan or ohio state. He was a standout in high school and had his pick of Big Ten scholarship offers. The

Denver post captured some stories about Lytle's recruitment to Michigan. Lytle stated in an interview with the Denver Post:

"I loved Woody, but there was something about Bo, He looks at me and says, 'You're not going to be any greater then you are right now.' But he says, 'When you sign with Michigan, you'll be the eighth-team tailback and whatever you do from that point is going to be an accomplishment for you. I have the firmest feeling that you can be the greatest running back that ever came out of Michigan.' That's what he told me. He lied to me. A guy quit, so I was the seventh-string tailback."

Bo wasn't handing a job to any player and Lytle knew he had to come to work. After minimal contributions as a freshman, Lytle started contributing regularly in 1974. He gained 802 yards as Gordon Bell's understudy that season, and had 10 touchdowns. As previously outlined Lytle provided a power option to Gordon Bell's speed and gave Bo Schembechler two great options at running back. During their years together Lytle even played fullback while Gordon was the tailback. In 1975 Lytle rushed for 1,043 yards to go along with 10 touchdowns.

Bell graduated, and Lytle was poised for a big senior year in 1976. The Wolverines won the Big Ten, but did drop a game at Purdue 16-14. With Lytle leading the way, the Wolverines were rolling. Other than the Purdue game, the Wolverines were dominant in the Big Ten in 1976. They beat Wisconsin in the season opener 40-27. Stanford, who they tied despite being heavy favorites in 1975 fell 51-0 to the Wolverines at the Big House. They beat rival Michigan State 42-10, and Lytle rushed for 180 yards on only 10 carries. They went to Evanston and beat Northwestern 38-7, with Lytle rushing for another 172 yards on 18 carries. The week after, the Wolverines went to Bloomington and beat Indiana 35-0. Lytle rushed for 25 times for 175 yards. Minnesota came to the Big House the next week, and Lytle and the Wolverines beat them 45-0. Lytle had 129 yards on 20 carries. The week after was the setback at Purdue, and

Michigan was ranked #1 when they went to West Lafayette. Lytle still had 153 yards, but Michigan fell to #4 in the polls. After the setback, the Wolverines got re-focused. They returned to the Big House and beat Illinois, 38-7. Lytle had only 89 yards rushing, but his two touchdowns set up a showdown with ohio state in the regular season finale.

They traveled to Columbus, and Lytle was up to the task. He carried the 29 times for 167 yards, and willed the Wolverines to a 22-0 victory over the #8 ranked buckeyes. It was their first win over ohio state since 1971. Oh the droughts. Michigan then played USC in the Rose Bowl, but fell 14-6. Lytle was held to 67 yards, and 3.9 yards per carry. As far as the Heisman Trophy voting went that year, Lytle finished 3rd. The winner was Tony Dorsett, the running back from Pittsburg. Ricky Bell of USC, who Lytle faced in his final game at Michigan in the Rose Bowl finished 2nd.

1976 HEISMAN VOTING RESULTS

PLACE	NAME	SCHOOL	CLASS	POSITION	1	2	3	TOTAL
1	TONY DORSETT	PITTSBURGH	SR.	RB	701	112	30	2357
2	RICKY BELL	USC	SR.	TB	73	485	157	1346
3	ROB LYTLE*	MICHIGAN	SR.	RB	35	85	138	413
4	TERRY MILLER	OKLAHOMA ST.	JR.	TB	18	43	57	197
5	TOMMY KRAMER	RICE	SR.	QB	6	7	31	63
6	GIFFORD NIELSEN	BYU	JR.	QB	1	7	28	45
7	RAY GOFF	GEORGIA	SR.	QB	2	12	14	44
8	MIKE VOIGHT	UNC	SR.	RB	1	7	24	41
9	JOE ROTH	CALIFORNIA	SR.	QB	0	6	20	32
10	JEFF DANKWORTH	UCLA	SR.	QB	2	6	13	31

As far as the *"THREE MICHIGAN HEISMAN CRITERIA"* relate to Lytle, he was Michigan Heisman material. Lytle was from Fremont, Ohio. He was a big time recruit and came to Michigan to play for Bo. Lastly, in his final game, he brought it home against the buckeyes, and the Wolverines won for the first time since 1971. He was Michigan's career rushing leader until the mark was broken by Jamie Morris in 1987.

After his career at Michigan, Lytle was drafted by the Denver Broncos in the 2nd round of the NFL Draft. He played seven seasons in Denver, and rushed for 1,451 yards. He also caught 61 passes for 562 yards. He accounted for 14 total NFL touchdowns with the Broncos, 12 rushing and 2 receiving. He was the first player in football history to score touchdowns in both the Super Bowl as a professional, and in the Rose Bowl as a collegiate player. Lytle's most memorable NFL moments came during the 1977 Broncos Super Bowl run. Lytle scored a touchdown against the Pittsburgh Steelers in the AFC Divisional playoff. The following game against the Oakland Raiders, Lytle fumbled as he dove for the end zone, but the play was blown dead. The Broncos went on to win the game, but fell to the Cowboys in Super Bowl XII. After football, Lytle and his family returned to Fremont, Ohio, where he had several business endeavors. He passed away November 20, 2010, of a heart attack at the age of 56.

1977-1978, RICK LEACH # 7

Rick Leach was born in Ann Arbor, Michigan. He was born at the University of Michigan Hospital, and his father and uncle both played baseball for the Wolverines. It was no surprise that this standout from Flint came to Michigan and played for Bo. He was 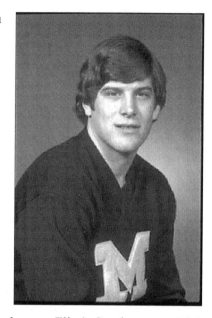 also a standout baseball player at Flint's Southwestern High School, and was reportedly offered a contract to play professional baseball before he ever arrived at Michigan. Schembechler outlined that he was open to Leach playing multiple sports at Michigan, which certainly aided in his decision to play college sports close to home. He played football, baseball, and even a little basketball as a freshman.

As a freshman in 1975, Leach became the first ever Michigan quarterback to start as a freshman. He paved the way for Chad Henne and Tate Forcier, and he did it under Bo Schembechler. Mark Elzinga was a senior, but for Schembechler, there was something about #7. He picked things up quickly. Despite never running the option, which was a big part of Michigan's offense in the 1970s, he learned quickly. The first game that year was at Wisconsin and Leach didn't know he was starting until they were in Badger country. Leach started and played the whole game. The results were mixed, but the Wolverines came away with a victory. He completed only 2 of 10 passes with 1 touchdown and 3 interceptions. On the ground, in the option offense, Leach ran for 30 yards on 8 carries. Remember though, that the freshman was sharing the backfield with Gordon Bell and Rob Lytle, and Bo knew he had some time to learn. That he did. Schembechler spoke about Leach several times, highlighting what a quick study he was. He learned things after the first time.

He held the position for the next 4 years at Michigan. He placed in the Heisman voting in both his junior season (8th, Earl Campbell was the winner) and senior seasons. In 1978 Leach led Michigan to a 10-2 record, the Big Ten title, and the Rose Bowl. The Wolverines fell to USC and Heisman candidate Charles White 17-10. Leach finished 3rd in the Heisman voting. Billy Sims, the running back from Oklahoma won the award, and Chuck Fusina, the Penn State quarterback finished second.

1978 HEISMAN VOTING RESULTS

PLACE	NAME	SCHOOL	CLASS	POSITION	1	2	3	TOTAL
1	BILLY SIMS	OKLAHOMA	JR.	RB	151	152	70	827
2	CHUCK FUSINA	PENN STATE	SR.	QB	163	89	83	750
3	RICK LEACH*	MICHIGAN	SR.	QB	89	58	52	435
4	CHARLES WHITE	USC	JR.	TB	36	74	98	354
5	CHARLES ALEXANDER	LSU	SR.	TB	42	51	54	282
6	TED BROWN	NC STATE	SR.	RB	5	19	29	82
7	STEVE FULLER	CLEMSON	SR.	QB	19	6	13	82
8	EDDIE LEE IVERY	GEORGIA TECH	SR.	RB	11	19	10	81
9	JACK THOMPSON	WASH STATE	SR.	QB	13	11	11	72
10	JERRY ROBINSON	UCLA	SR.	LB	12	11	12	70

Along with Gordon Bell and Rob Lytle, Leach battled Griffin during his second Heisman campaign. Leach finished his Michigan career as the all-time leading passer for the Wolverines. He passed for 4,284 yards 48 touchdowns with 35 interceptions. He also rushed for 2,176 yards and 34 more touchdowns. Of the *"THREE MICHIGAN HEISMAN CRITERIA,"* Leach was two for three. He was a big time recruit, brought it home against the buckeyes in 1978, but was also from the great state of Michigan.

After Michigan, Leach chose professional baseball. In 1979, Leach was selected in the first round of the Major League Baseball amateur draft by, you guessed it, the Detroit Tigers. He was also drafted by the Denver Broncos in 1979. During his 10 year career, Leach played for the Detroit Tigers, Toronto Blue Jays, Texas Rangers, and San Francisco Giants. Leach was born a **MICHIGAN MAN.**

1980-1982, ANTHONY CARTER # 1

Anthony Carter was born in Riviera Beach, FL. Bo Schembechler and his staff recruited him out of Sun Coast High School. The offense at the time relied heavily on running backs, but Michigan pursued

the smallish Carter. He was around 5'11" and 160 pounds. Common sense would say that Carter was not Big Ten power football material. Bo thought otherwise. Not only did he make an offer to Anthony Carter, but he assigned him the #1 Jersey, and a Michigan tradition was soon to be born. In 1979, in the season opener against Northwestern, "AC" made an immediate impact. He returned a punt 78 yards for a touchdown. Carter continued to play well as a freshman, and made the most of his opportunities. His 45 yard game winning touchdown catch against Indiana as time ran out might be the greatest play in Michigan Football history. Bob Ufer's play by play call sealed Carter's place forever.

Although Carter only had 17 receptions for the season, 7 were for touchdowns. He averaged 27.2 yards per catch. Additionally, Carter returned kickoffs in addition to punts.

Over the next 3 years, "AC" would become a Michigan legend. He placed in the Heisman voting in 1980 (10th) and 1981 (7th), and he was re-writing the Michigan receiving and return record books. In 1982, as a senior, Carter and Wolverines went 8-4. Despite the "disappointing" season, Carter finished 4th in the Heisman Trophy voting. You may have heard of the guys that finished 1-3, Herschel Walker, John Elway, and Eric Dickerson.

1982 HEISMAN TROPHY VOTING RESULTS

PLACE	NAME	SCHOOL	CLASS	POSITION	1	2	3	TOTAL
1	HERSCHEL WALKER	GEORGIA	JR.	TB	525	155	41	1926
2	JOHN ELWAY	STANFORD	SR.	QB	139	335	144	1231
3	ERIC DICKERSON	SMU	SR.	TB	31	100	172	465
4	ANTHONY CARTER*	MICHIGAN	SR.	WR	11	27	55	142
5	DAVID REMINGTON	NEBRASKA	SR.	C	13	23	52	137
6	TODD BLACKLEDGE	PENN STATE	SR.	QB	4	26	44	108
7	TOM RAMSEY	UCLA	SR.	QB	2	16	27	65
8	TONY EATON	ILLINOIS	SR.	QB	5	6	33	60
9	DAN MARINO	PITTSBURGH	SR.	QB	1	6	32	47
10	MIKE ROZIER	NEBRASKA	JR.	RB	4	8	12	40
11	CURT WARNER	PENN STATE	SR.	TB	2	8	18	40

When Carter left Michigan, he was the Wolverine's all-time leader in receptions, receiving yards, touchdown receptions, punt returns, punt return yards, kickoff returns, and kickoff return yardage. His 3,076 receiving yards is still second best in Michigan history. As a senior, "AC" was also named the Conference Player of the year, and he was an All American. As for the

"THREE MICHIGAN HEISMAN CRITERIA," Carter was unique. He was the first Michigan Heisman candidate from way outside the Midwest. I personally think that Florida as a rival state, but he definitely didn't come from the Midwest. Secondly, Bo took a chance bringing this electric but small talent to Ann Arbor. Lastly, despite re-writing the Michigan record books, and setting the tradition of the #1 Jersey at Michigan, Carter's teams were 1-3 against ohio state. Until 2008, the #1 Jersey was given to Michigan's top receivers as a reward. Greg McMurtry, Derrick Alexander, David Terrell, and Braylon Edwards all wore the #1 Jersey, originally given to and worn by Anthony Carter. If the tradition hadn't started, Carter's jersey would certainly have been retired. In 2011, Michigan Head Coach Brady

Hoke said that the tradition will be revived in the years to come.

After Michigan, Carter took his immense talents to the USFL instead of the NFL, where he played for the Michigan Panthers. The Panthers won the USFL Championship in 1983, and Carter caught a 48 yard touchdown to win the game. Carter remained in the USFL through 1985, and then signed with the Miami Dolphins in the NFL. Before taking the field for the Dolphins, "AC" was traded to the Minnesota Vikings. Carter played for the Vikings from 1983 until 1993. He made the Pro Bowl in 1987 and 1988. His Viking teams were successful. In 1994 and 1995, Carter joined the Detroit Lions. He was attempting to overcome injuries where it all started. Carter played little in 1994 and 1995, after which he retired. Carter played 11 total seasons in the NFL, and finished with 7,733 receiving yards and 55 touchdowns. For a 5'11", 160 pound recruit, Carter made the most of his talents and opportunities. Bo sure could spot a **MICHIGAN MAN** when he saw one. Carter resides in Florida and runs the Anthony Carter Jr Foundation which fights Cerebral Palsy, a disease that his son is battling.

1986, JIM HARBAUGH # 4

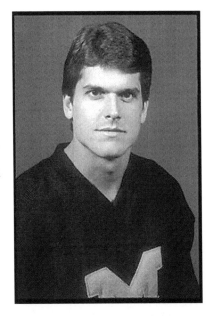

James Joseph "Jim" Harbaugh was born just down Highway 23 from the Big House in Toledo, Ohio. He played youth football, and then middle school football at Tappan Junior High in Ann Arbor. From there, he played at Ann Arbor Pioneer High School. His father, Jack Harbaugh was an assistant coach on Bo Schembechler's Michigan staff from 1973-1979, coaching the defensive backs. The family moved to Palo Alto, California in 1980, when Jack accepted a job as Stanford's defensive coordinator. Jim finished his career at Palo Alto High School. He was a high school player with options. Stanford was across the street at the time, and Michigan was the source of several great memories. During some very impressionable years, Harbaugh would attend practice with his father, practices run by Bo. The family didn't return to Ann Arbor for the two years that Jim finished his High School career, and to his knowledge, he was being

RECRUITED by Stanford, Arizona, Wisconsin, and some other big time programs. Although he wanted to be at Michigan, he received little interest. In 1982, Harbaugh even arranged a meeting with Schembechler while he was in town coaching the East-West Shrine game. Harbaugh left the meeting mostly disappointed, but would eventually be offered a scholarship. Bo was tough on Harbaugh, even during the recruiting process.

Once he arrived in Ann Arbor, Bo never let up. He and his quarterback would battle on and off the field, and that tough love made Harbaugh into one of the greatest quarterbacks in Michigan history. Bo was hard on the cocky young gunslinger, maybe the hardest. Bo's challenges made him restrain his nature in order to become a more effective player and leader. The fiery competitiveness that made Harbaugh who he was, often found him on the wrong side of his legendary coach. As he developed into the quarterback that Bo knew he could be, over time Michigan fans certainly got to enjoy the results.

I told you up front that I am a lifelong Michigan fan, and my first memories of Michigan Football are from the Harbaugh era. I was 6 in 1984. I wouldn't say I was quite a Michigan "Fan" yet, but the interest was growing. At that age I was very busy. I was GI Joe, an aspiring professional wrestler, and more than determined to beat Mike Tyson in Punchout! (007-373-5963 will give you your chance). My memory worked even before I started automatically logging box scores. Even during those times however, I couldn't help notice what my Dad was doing on Saturdays. There was a game on, one game, each week. Of course he would watch others when he could, but with five kids things were busy.

He was teaching ROTC at the University of Michigan, and one day a 5'7" Michigan running back came to the ROTC Department with questions. His name was Jamie Morris. Morris was an Army brat, and needed to update his Military ID card. On his current path, who thought he would need it, but I think Jamie knew the power of the "PX" or Post Exchange. The "PX" is the Wal-Mart of the military world, everything you could ever want, but at an incredible discount. So my father, with 5 kids to entertain with my Mom, struck a deal. On a weekend trip to the "BX" at Selfridge Air Force Base (it's the Base Exchange in the Air Force) our guest was Jamie Morris. Later visits to the Gallagher home brought some of his teammates, to include Phil Webb, another Michigan running back. For any buckeyes who accidentally stumble upon this story listen up. If you are looking for tattoos and allegations, the Gallaghers can't help you. If riding in our family conversion van with the curtains, ruby lights, checkerboard, and Huey Lewis blasting is an allegation then we will certainly talk to the NCAA. My Mom fed Michigan's all-purpose yards career leader, and that is it. Coming from a big family himself I think he related to us. So no dirt, no benefits, just some time away from class and football, and the beginning of my lifelong career as a Michigan fan. In elementary school, I received a "physical fitness" award. I can't quite remember what the criteria were (tying shoes and breathing?), but the presenters were Jim Harbaugh and Jamie Morris. So as my Dad continued to watch, I was looking for the guys I met and learning about the game.

After some early ups and downs, Bo handed the reins to Harbaugh in 1984, his sophomore season. Michigan started strong, defeating the #1 ranked Miami Hurricanes at the Big House. Bernie Kosar (4th in the Heisman Voting in 1984) was the quarterback for the Hurricanes, but Harbaugh stole the spotlight in his first start. He completed 11/21 passes for 163 yards. Although he threw two interceptions, like Leach, he also had plenty of help. The Michigan defense intercepted Kosar 6 times. After defeating the Hurricanes, Michigan hosted Washington the following week. # 4 never got the luxury of a warm up game. Michigan lost to Washington 20-11, and Jim continued to learn under fire. He threw his first touchdown pass in the game, but also threw 3 interceptions. Michigan won the next two games against Wisconsin and Indiana, and Harbaugh was improving. He threw touchdowns in each game, and did not throw an interception. On October 6th, 1984, Michigan traveled to East Lansing to play the Spartans. He started the game strong. He completed 7/14 passes for 101 yards. Then Michigan's 1984 season would hit a significant road block. In the third quarter, Jamie Morris took a handoff from Harbaugh, got hit, and fumbled the ball. While attempting to recover the fumble, he broke his left arm in the scramble. In the Gallagher household, October 6th, 1984 was a rough one. Michigan State went on to win 19-7, and the Wolverines finished with a 6-6 record after losing to BYU in the Holiday Bowl.

Harbaugh recovered, and when Michigan took the field in 1985, they were unranked but motivated to correct the meltdown of 1984. With their quarterback under center, the 1985 season started at the Big House against Notre Dame. Backed by defense and strong running game, Michigan beat Notre Dame 20-12, and with a healthy Harbaugh, Michigan was starting to roll. They would start the season 5-0, and against rival Michigan State, #4 avenged the 1984 setback. Although he threw 3 interceptions in the game, he also threw 2 touchdowns, and the Wolverines were heading to Iowa City, undefeated, and ranked #2. The Hawkeyes were ranked #1. In a hard fought battle, Iowa would prevail, 12-10, on a last second field goal by Iowa kicker Rob Houghtlin. The 1985 Wolverines wouldn't lose another game. On November 2nd, 1985, Michigan tied a stingy Illinois team 3-3 in Champaign, and from there they ran the table. Harbaugh was making his mark with games of 283, 233, and 243 yards passing in Big Ten play. Michigan was throwing the ball, and Schembechler was even smiling. In the season finale against ohio state, #4 shined. In the 27-17 win at the Big House, he had his best game to date at Michigan completing 16/19 passes for 230 yards, 3 touchdowns and no interceptions. The Wolverines beat Nebraska in the Fiesta Bowl, and were ready for a big season in 1986. During his junior year, Jim Harbaugh led the nation in passing efficiency.

Once again, Michigan opened with Notre Dame, at South Bend. They were ranked #2 in the Nation. In a 24-23 victory, he continued where he left off in 1985. With the nation watching, he completed 15/23 passes for 239 yards, 1 touchdown and no interceptions. Michigan would start the season 8-0, and within the confines of a talented Michigan team, Harbaugh was putting on a show. At Wisconsin in week 4, he would become Michigan's first quarterback ever to throw for 300 yards in a single game. He went 15/24, for 310 yards with 1 touchdown and 0 interceptions. The Wolverines kept rolling. He threw for 219 yards against Michigan State, and 2 more touchdowns. In the rematch with Iowa, that ended on a last second field goal and knocked Michigan out of National Title contention in 1985, the roles were reversed in 1986.

In Michigan stadium, where I sat with my Mom and Dad, it was the Wolverines who had the ball last. Harbaugh

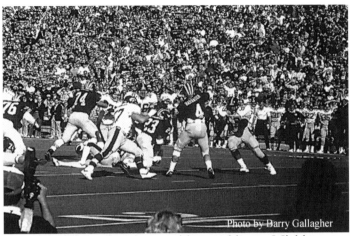

Photo by Barry Gallagher

moved the Wolverines into position, and it was Michigan kicker Mike Gillette splitting the uprights as time expired.

At Indiana the next week, he would have the second 300 yard passing game in Michigan History as the Wolverines won big. Toward the end of the first half, there was a play that I feel perfectly defined Harbaugh's career at Michigan and relationship with Bo Schembechler. With the game already in hand, #4 rolled out to the right and his receivers were covered. The scrambling ability that sometimes drove Bo crazy was about to make a big play. The opportunity to throw the ball away and set up a field goal wasn't on Jim's agenda. He spun away from trouble and changed his launch location from the right sideline to the left sideline where he threw a deep pass to #31 Kenny Higgins for a touchdown. Following the game, on Michigan

Replay, the Highlight of the Game was dissected by Coach Schembechler. During the weekly show, Bo declared "It was a broken play... As Jim Brandstatter, the host of Michigan Replay announced the "Budweiser Play of the Game" you could almost hear Bo's Smirk:

"Jim, this is the broken play of the game, this is not one you design, not one coaches brag about, or talk about... this is a bomb thrown down there before the half, and Kenny Higgins is able to catch it, it's a big play for the fans, but it is a broken play."

Wolverine great Jim Harbaugh had a much different memory of the play during the same Michigan Replay Episode:

"I thought it was great though, just a great job by Kenny Higgins of getting open, he had a man on his back, and just started turning and running for the end zone and I saw him and just really let it loose, as far as I could throw it, and ah, just fortunately he caught it, I will remember that one for a long time."

Looking back at the Episode, it made me laugh to see Harbaugh's journey from a son on the practice field to an NFL quarterback summarized by the different accounts that he and Bo had for the very same play. The Wolverines kept rolling with #4 under center until Minnesota came to town. The # 2 ranked Wolverines may have taken their opponent lightly, and a fleet footed quarterback named Ricky Foggie made them pay. The Wolverines were sluggish all day and turned the ball over 5 times. Foggie capitalized with a touchdown pass and a touchdown run. Long time NFL kicker Chip Lohmiller kicked a 30 yard field goal at the end that ended the Wolverines National Title aspirations. The tough loss overshadowed the milestones for Harbaugh on that day. His 207 yards set marks for passing yards in a season at Michigan, and he also became the school's all-time leading passer. Michigan fell to #6 in the rankings.

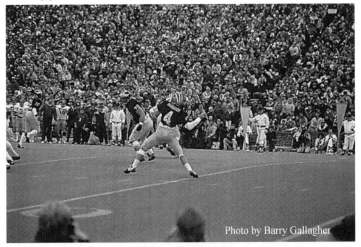

Photo by Barry Gallagher

A disappointed team headed to ohio stadium the following week and Harbaugh had no problem motivating his team. In the 83rd matchup of the biggest rivalry in College Football, the fireworks began long before the teams took the field. During the Monday news conference, he shared:

"I guarantee we will beat Ohio State and be in Pasadena on New Year's Day. People don't give us a snowball's chance in hell to beat them in Columbus, but we're going to do it. We don't care where we play the game. I hate to say it, but we could play it in the parking lot. We could play at twelve noon or midnight. We're going to be jacked up."

Following his lead, the Wolverines backed those words. In an even matchup, Michigan prevailed 26-24. Harbaugh passed for 261 yards, but also threw 2 interceptions. Jamie Morris and the line gave plenty of support however, with Morris rushing for 210 yards. The 10th place vote receiver for the Heisman in 1986 was none other than buckeye linebacker Chris Spielman. With 1:02 left in the game, ohio state's kicker missed a 45 yard field goal. If we could only know exactly what Bo was thinking when Harbaugh let his media grenade fly.... It's what we see weekly in the world of "Tweeter," but not from Bo's quarterback. Michigan had a rare game after ohio state at Hawaii, and after that victory they headed to the Rose Bowl as their quarterback predicted. The Wolverines fell 22-15 to Arizona State, and #4 struggled with 3 interceptions. Harbaugh would finish 3rd in the Heisman Trophy voting with Vinny Testaverde, quarterback of the Miami Hurricanes the winner.

1986 HEISMAN VOTING RESULTS

PLACE	NAME	SCHOOL	CLASS	POSITION	1	2	3	TOTAL
1	VINNY TESTAVERDE	MIAMI	SR.	QB	678	76	27	2213
2	PAUL PALMER	TEMPLE	SR.	TB	28	207	174	672
3	JIM HARBAUGH*	MICHIGAN	SR.	QB	25	136	111	458
4	BRIAN BOSWORTH	OKLAHOMA	JR.	LB	9	136	96	395
5	GORDON LOCKBAUM	HOLY CROSS	JR.	TB-DB	32	39	68	242
6	BRENT FULLWOOD	AUBURN	SR.	TB	4	45	27	129
7	CORNELIUS BENNETT	ALABAMA	SR.	LB	3	29	29	96
8	D.J. DOZIER	PENN STATE	SR.	TB	0	23	31	77
9	KEVIN SWEENEY	FRESNO STATE	SR.	QB	6	16	23	73
10	CHRIS SPIELMAN	OHIO STATE	JR.	LB	5	9	27	60

As for the ***"THREE MICHIGAN HEISMAN CRITERIA,"*** Harbaugh is a challenge to rate. Although he came to Michigan after living in Pac 10 country, it's hard to claim he was from enemy territory based on his ties with Bo and Michigan. He was a big time recruit, and came through on a victory guarantee against the buckeyes at ohio stadium as senior. He finished 2-0 in the games against osu the he played in during his career. He left as Michigan's career passing leader with 5,449 yards. Currently, Harbaugh is ranked #4, and his 2,729 yards in 1986 is still the 4th best in Wolverine history. He will always be the man, who enticed Bo Schembechler let it fly from time to time.

After Michigan, he moved on to the NFL. Michigan's all-time leading passer was drafted by the Chicago Bears in the first round at the 26th pick. His first NFL coach would be Mike Ditka, and I don't think there was anyone more prepared after his four years of tough love from Bo. Who else can say they received so many benefits from getting yelled at by two of the greatest coaches in the history of football? Even the draft selection stirred up controversy. The Bears already had an ailing Jim McMahon in addition to Doug Flutie, Steve Fuller, and Mike Tomczack on the roster. People were concerned how the veterans would take it, but I know Harbaugh wasn't one of them.

He spent 7 total seasons with Bears, and the Gallagher family moved to Chicago in 1989 for my Dad's next Army assignment. From 1994-1997, Jim played for the Indianapolis Colts. During the 1995-1996 NFL season Harbaugh was back in the lime light. He was named the NFL Comeback Player of the Year, and finished second in the MVP voting. The Colts fell to the Pittsburg Steelers in the AFC Championship game, when #4 threw a last second Hail Mary that rolled off of receiver Aaron Bailey's chest. That game broke my heart like a Michigan loss. Not only was I happy for Harbaugh and his comeback, but the guy who watched the Super Bowl roll off his chest ran track with my oldest brother Mike at Ann Arbor Pioneer High School. The small world connection is yet another example of why sports amaze me.

Harbaugh retired from the NFL after 2001 and continues to put his mark on football as a successful Head Coach. He recently left Stanford to coach the 49ers in the

NFL. Jim broke the hearts of Michigan fans in 2011, when it was rumored he would take the Head Coaching job prior to accepting the position in the NFL. Even with that, this **MICHIGAN MAN** never has been one to do what is expected. He still has the flair, just ask his opponents. The man now leading the 49ers will tell you who is going to win. In his first NFL season as a Head Coach, he even went head to head with his brother. It hasn't taken long and the 49ers are already looking like a contender again, and as a Rookie Coach he took them to the NFC Championship Game.

21

DESMOND HOWARD
MAGIC AT THE BIG HOUSE

Desmond Kevin Howard was born in Cleveland, Ohio on May 15th, 1970. His parents worked hard, his father in a tool and die shop and his mother ran a day care from home. At the age of 13, his parents split up, and Desmond would live with his Dad. It wasn't a case where his father "won" because there is no such thing in a split. Instead it was a decision made and in the process his mother went back to school to receive her college degree. His father even took on more hours in order to provide Desmond the opportunity to attend a private high school.

I can relate. Being one of five kids, I can tell you that my parents worked hard and do to this day. Despite being a Major in the United States Army while we lived in Chicago, my Dad was delivering the USA Today out of our family van early in the morning to help my oldest brother Mike with his wedding, and my mother has run a day care from home, managed the office for two successful dentists,' and now works as a special education teacher in Illinois. A parent's love is amazing, and I believe Howard would agree. So it came time for high school, and the aspiring student athlete picked St. Joseph's Academy known for discipline, academics, and sports. His father, J.D. even made a deal with him prior to his sophomore year, challenging him to concentrate on his academic and athletic endeavors. He challenged him to socialize less, leave the girls alone, and concentrate on school and sports. Desmond responded. I wonder how I would of reacted if my Dad laid down the same challenge, but to Howard's credit, he did it. After practices, he come home and ran. During the prom, he ran in a track meet. Finally as a senior, J.D.'s words were coming to fruition.

During his final high school season, the running back/defensive back from St. Joseph's Academy scored 18 touchdowns and also recorded 10 interceptions. More than 20 schools were recruiting the son of J.D. and Hattie Howard, and one of them was Michigan. Gary Moeller, a Michigan assistant at the time, was handling Howard's recruitment. I don't know who he saw first, but there was another player from St. Joseph's academy who came to Michigan with Howard. His name was Elvis Grbac, the quarterback. A guy who started playing football when he was recruited off the basketball team by an athletic young man with a big smile, was also on his way to Michigan. ohio state was one of the other schools in contention, but they were also going through a coaching change and had just hired a guy named John Cooper. Howard thought there was certainly some uncertainty in Columbus, Ohio. So despite several options, Desmond was a Wolverine, and arrived in 1988. His hometown of Cleveland, Ohio was 139 miles from ohio stadium, and 166 to the Big House.

When practice began, this running back/defensive back from Cleveland was working with the defensive backs.

Coach Moeller asked him what he was doing, and Desmond's response outlined that he wanted to play as soon as possible. After some deliberation between Schembechler and Moeller, Howard moved to wide receiver, where he would remain for the rest of his career. He spent his first year at Michigan practicing but did not earn a varsity letter. The initial change took time. Howard struggled with coaching and the position change but would eventually rise to the top. Howard took the field for the Wolverines in 1989. He played sparingly during his freshman season, but he did play. Michigan had two talented and experienced receivers in #1 Greg McMurtry and #2 Chris Calloway.

In the season opener against # 1 ranked Notre Dame, Howard caught 1 pass for 6 yards, and also returned 2 kickoffs for 62 yards for the #2 ranked Wolverines. Not bad for a freshman, but for Notre Dame a guy named Rocket Ismail was putting on a show. "The Rocket" did what no man had done to Michigan in 32 years, and to make it worse he did it twice. He returned two kickoffs for touchdowns, one for 88 yards and the other for 92. I can't help but wonder what Desmond might have been thinking watching the "Rocket" takeoff. Confident and competitive, I am sure Howard was upset that the Wolverines were down. On the other hand though, I think Desmond knew his day would come. Ismail, like Howard was lightning in cleats. He was also similar in stature at 5'10," 175 pounds. Howard was listed at 5'10," 172 pounds as a freshman and I think it was 5'9". Neither the Rocket nor Desmond are supposed to survive in College Football. The only problem is you have to catch them first.

During his freshman season, Howard recorded 9 catches, but amazingly two went for touchdowns. He even played in the 1990 Rose Bowl game, where he missed a touchdown opportunity when the pass intended for him was overthrown. Michigan would fall 17-10 in last game coached by the legendary Bo Schembechler. By the time I watched that disappointment with my Dad, I was started to feel the emotions of the game. A late holding call on a successful fake punt doomed the Wolverines. That was the first

Michigan loss that I felt in my stomach, and I was certainly getting hooked. So when a young Desmond Howard and the Wolverines looked toward 1990, he was determined to make an impact. Gary Moeller, Bo's long-time assistant became the Head Coach. Bo left the cupboard anything but bare, and Michigan came into the season

ranked #6 in the Associated Press Poll. With an early season
schedule left over from Bo, before the move to play all the
directional Michigans, the Wolverines would open with
Notre Dame. That is no slight to the Eagles, Chippewas, or
Broncos. Heck my sister is a Bronco, but come on people,
one game to work out the bugs wasn't Bo's way. It was no
mistake that Michigan was ranked highly heading into the
matchup with Notre Dame. In addition to a sophomore
burner named Desmond Howard at one receiver, Derrick
Alexander, another big time receiver from Detroit was on the
other side. An experienced offensive line anchored by Greg
Skrepenak, Matt Elliot, and Steve Everitt was poised to open
holes for a loaded backfield to include Jon Vaughn, Ricky
Powers, and Jarod Bunch. Howard was familiar with his
quarterback. It was none other than Elvis Grbac his high
school teammate. Grbac actually received significant
playing time in 1989 when Michael Taylor was injured. The
defense was also loaded, with experience, depth, and an All
American defensive back named Trip Welbourne. Michigan
was ranked # 4 when they went to South Bend for the
matchup with #1 ranked Notre Dame. No, that is not a typo,
Michigan moved up two spots before they even played a
game.

Rick Mirer was Notre Dame's quarterback, and his
favorite target was once again Heisman Trophy Candidate
(finishing 2nd in 1990) the "Rocket" Raghib Ismail. In 1990

however, Howard was ready to duel. Although Notre Dame would eventually win the game, Michigan came to play. Howard would catch a total of 6 passes for 133 yards and 2 touchdowns, and tailback Jon Vaughn became an early Heisman rumor after his 22 rush, 201 yard performance slashing through the Notre Dame defense. Michigan held a 24-14 lead after Howard's second touchdown catch in the 3rd quarter. Late in the game however, Rick Mirer connected on an 8 yard touchdown pass to Adrian Jarrell to win the game. Michigan fell to #7 in the rankings, but had displayed two new offensive weapons that would have to be dealt with in 1990.

Michigan faced UCLA in their second game and won big on another huge performance by the offensive line and the nation's leading rusher Jon Vaughn. Vaughn rushed 32 times for 288 yards and 3 touchdowns. Michigan didn't need to pass much, but Howard still managed 4 catches for 46 yards. He also had 73 yards on 2 kickoff returns for a 36.5 yard average. The next week brought Maryland to the Big House, and Michigan kept rolling. In the 45-17 victory Michigan was able to spread the ball around and Howard scored another touchdown.

The Big Ten opener in 1990 for the Wolverines was at Wisconsin. Michigan was ranked #3, while Wisconsin was unranked. A focused Wolverine team, with a balanced attack under Moeller overpowered Wisconsin 41-3, and the

5'9" receiver from Cleveland Ohio added two more touchdowns. I guess he had taken to WR just fine.

In week five, it was rivalry time once again. The Spartans came to the Big House for the annual battle of the State of Michigan and the Paul Bunyan Trophy. Michigan was ranked #1. Notre Dame and Florida State dropped games to Stanford and Miami, and the Wolverines jumped up from #3. The Spartans came to play on October 13th, 1990 as in state rivals always do. In an even matchup, the score was tied at 14 in the 4th quarter. At that point, things got interesting. Michigan State tailback Hyland Hickson scored on a memorable 26 yard run to include a video game spin move with 6:03 remaining to quiet the crowd in the Big House. The Spartans kicked off to you guessed it, Desmond Howard, and he was about to showcase another phase of his growing game. Howard caught the kickoff around the 5 yard line, and as the Big House crowd roared, he headed up the left sideline with a convoy of Wolverines. Past mid-field Howard cut back, leaving Spartans in his wake and RACED to the right side of the end zone. It was an indicator of things to come from Howard, and the Wolverines tied the game. His teammates mobbed him in the end zone. The Spartans would respond again. Hickson extended the ensuing drive, this time on a pass from Dan Enos, and the Spartans were on the move. Tico Duckett, the other talented Spartans back scored on a 9 yard run with around 4 minutes remaining in the game. Like I said, things were getting interesting. The Wolverines would drive back. In a methodical drive, Michigan quarterback Elvis Grbac would utilize multiple receivers, marching the Wolverines back down the field. Desmond Howard caught a Grbac pass to advance Michigan to the Michigan State 8 yard line. Grbac found Derrick Alexander on a fade/stop route with 6 seconds left and the Wolverines trailed 28-27. Gary Moeller was not looking to tie the score. The Wolverines went for 2. With Alexander to the right side, and Howard to the left, Grbac dropped back and threw a slant pass to Desmond, falling into the end zone. He caught the ball momentarily and it came loose when he hit the ground. He was falling because he was tripped by Spartan defensive back Eddie Brown. Fans were on the field, Michigan was looking for the interference flag, and it even looked like Howard may have had control on the catch anyway. No luck. The Wolverines even recovered an onside kick to have one more heave toward the end zone, but the pass would be intercepted, and the Spartans victory over #1 ranked Michigan will always be remembered for the controversy associated with it, at least to us Michigan fans. On www.msuspartans.com, a recap of the game was posted on October 30th, 2007, and simply states "but Grbac's two-point conversion pass to Howard fell incomplete in the end zone, preserving MSU's victory." Come on Sparty, how do you sleep at night? In addition to the kickoff return, Howard caught 8 passes for 140 yards on the day, but if he could only have another shot at that two point conversion...

Michigan would face another set back the following week against Iowa for the Homecoming game, but would win out from there. Desmond Howard continued to make a name for himself as one of the best receivers in the Big Ten, and on November 24th, 1990, the converted running back / defensive back from Cleveland would get his first real shot against the ohio state buckeyes. Although Howard would be held to 73 yards receiving on 5 catches, as usual, he made them count. A tradition had caught on in the Big Ten by the time Michigan traveled to Columbus, and the buckeyes joined in. In the ultimate sign of fear and respect, teams weren't kicking to ball to #21.

I graduated from high school in St. Louis and used to go see the Cardinals play baseball. Sports are about winning and strategy, and there is a simple rule that you sometimes have to follow. Don't give them a chance to burn you. This book isn't about steroids and baseball. Think what you want, but I would go watch a guy who could kill a baseball. You didn't pitch to Mark McGwire and you didn't kick to Desmond Howard. Derrick Alexander did make some big returns against the buckeyes in 1990 (3 for 82 yards) but Desmond would have to make his impact elsewhere. In the third quarter of a tight game, Desmond did just that. He caught a 14 yard slant for a touchdown and the Wolverines would prevail 16-13.

On January 1ˢᵗ 1991, my love for Michigan, and the sport of football officially took its' course. I had watched the Nationally Televised games in 1990, but in life before the Big Ten Network and the College Football package, I missed several games. For the first time in my life, I anxiously awaited the bowl season, and Michigan's matchup with the University of Mississippi. Of course my father was watching with me, but it was me that had the VCR rolling, ready for kickoff. This was the first incident of VCR wars in the Gallagher household, and the lines were drawn. My brother Mike was off to West Point, so it was my parents, two brothers, and my sister at home. We lived in the suburbs of Chicago in a place called Wheaton. There were 3 TV's in the house, but only one VCR. Only two of us really used the VCR outside of family movie night, me and my older sister Wendy. Wendy taped soap operas, movies, ice skating, and shows. I taped sports, lots of sports. So in desperation the morning of the game, I declared war. The tape, ~~*Anne of Avonlee*~~ *1991 Mazda Gator Bowl* went into the VCR, and I settled in for the game. The battle would rage on for years. I won some, I lost some. Oh the rage however when I put in the 1990 Pistons finals games and found figure skating.

~~1990 PISTONS STUFF~~ US FIGURE SKATING CHAMPIONSHIPS

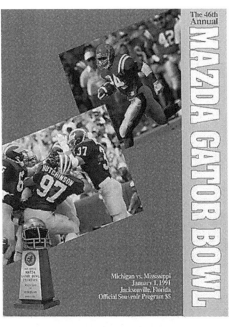

You have to understand that Wendy was the only girl, and she had no choice but to be tough. We still laugh about it to this day, and I still have my tapes, that I have been dragging around since. So although I started a war, the 1991 Mazda Gator Bowl was worth it. Michigan took a 7-0 lead on a touchdown pass from Elvis Grbac to none other than Desmond Howard, and I was starting to see what the nation wouldn't figure out until the 1991 season. The play action pass covered 63 yards. The pass was actually under thrown, and two Mississippi defensive backs closed in on Desmond, who had to stop to catch the ball. He caught it, accelerated, and stepped out of two attempted ankle tackles, his feet just simply too fast. Howard caught other passes in the first half, and returned a kickoff to the 30 yard line, with only a shoe string tackle preventing him from going all the way. On that play, I remember watching Howard's reaction, despite a good return. He was shaking his head, and thinking about what should have happened, he thought he should have scored. Although I was a Michigan fan prior to the 1991 Mazda Gator Bowl, on that day I saw something special in #21.

I saw electricity that I wanted to have. I hadn't really had a "favorite" player since Harbaugh and Morris, but Desmond was making up my mind. Michigan led 14-3 at halftime, and the show had just begun. On the first drive of the second half, Howard took a handoff on a reverse and raced for 15 more yards. Later in the 3rd quarter, Howard caught an out pass on a blitz, no more than 8 yards down the

1991 MAZDA GATOR BOWL

First Quarter			Wolverines		Rebels
			35	First Downs	20
M	Howard, 63-yard pass from Grbac (Carlson kick)		391	Net Yards Rushing	93
			324	Net Yards Passing	215
Second Quarter			85	Total Plays	67
			715	Total Yards	306
MS	Lee, 51-yard field goal		32/20/2	PA/PC/Int	31/17/4
	Bunch, 7-yard pass from Grbac (Carlson kick)		2/24.5	Punts/Avg.	6/38.0
M			65	Return Yards	192
			2/1	Fumbles/Lost	4/2
Third Quarter			6/69	Penalties/Yards	4/49
M	Howard, 50-yard pass from Grbac (Carlson kick)				
M	Bunch, 5-yard run (Carlson kick)				
M	Alexander, 33-yard pass from Grbac (Carlson kick)				

Rushing– (M): Vaughn, 15-128; Powers, 14-112; Bunch, 11-54; Legette, 5-54; Howard, 1-19; Washington, 3-15; Watson, 1-5; Jefferson, 3-4; (MS): Baldwin, 8-53; Thigpen, 6-32; Billing, 2-6; Courtney, 1-6; Luke, 14-5; Shows, 5-(-9)

Passing– (M): Grbac, 16-25-296; Sollom, 4-7-28; (MS): Shows, 12-20-150; Luke, 5-11-65

Receiving– (M:): Howard, 6-167; Alexander, 2-50; VanDyne, 3-32; Bunch, 2-22; Burch, 1-12; Vaughn, 1-10; Owen, 1-9; Powers, 1-8; Johnson, 2-7; Diebolt, 1-7; (MS) Roberts, 4-67; Brownlee, 4-59; Owens, 3-42; Small, 1-25; Baldwin, 2-15; Holder, 1-11; Thigpen, 1-6; Courtney, 1-3

MICHIGAN 35, OLE MISS 3

field. Howard turned on the brakes and instead of heading out of bounds he spun back to the middle, juked one defender and raced past the entire Mississippi defense to include 2 safeties with angles. The ESPN announcers were raving how much Howard reminded them of Anthony Carter and I was realizing that this guy could score on ANY play. Another play action pass, and Howard was wide open again, 30 more yards. Howard finished the game with 6 catches for 167 yards and two touchdowns receiving. I was hooked, and Michigan was poised for a big year in 1991. Howard was named All-Big Ten as a sophomore, but wasn't garnering a lot of attention outside the Big Ten conference. That was about to change.

With my mind made up, I was Desmond all summer long. My older brother Mark and I spent a lot of time throwing the football. Wherever we were, home, the family cottage in Michigan, or at rest areas across the Midwest on family road trips, my request to Mark was simple. Throw me a Grbac fade route, somewhere I can dive for it. Michigan was ranked #3 in the nation, and I anxiously awaited the start of the season. I knew it was going to be a big year for Michigan, and especially for #21.

Michigan was loaded in 1991, just like 1990. Despite losing some good players to include safety Trip Welbourne, tackle Tom Dohring, running back Jon Vaughn, fullback Jarrod Bunch, and guard Dean Dingman Michigan had plenty of talent and experience. Moeller and Michigan had to be excited about who they were taking to Boston College for the season opener on September 7th, 1991. Desmond Howard picked right up where he left off in the Gator Bowl, and dazzled the Boston College crowd. Howard would account for all 4 Michigan touchdowns on the day for the offense, with the 5th coming on a Lance Dottin interception return to seal the game. Another event happened in Chesnutt Hill on that day. Howard's teammate and other star receiver Derrick Alexander would be lost to a

knee injury for the season. Most outside of Michigan don't remember that injury, but I think it was a key-event that changed the course of Michigan and Desmond Howard's season and pushed the door a little further open for a Heisman run. In the 2nd quarter against Boston College, Howard caught a 19 yard touchdown pass to put the Wolverines on the board against the upset minded Eagles. To start the second half, Boston College either got brave or forgot about the McGwire rule I outlined previously, and Desmond made them pay. He received the opening kickoff of the 2nd half and 93 yards later, he was in the end zone again. The game stayed close, but in the 4th quarter, #21 would catch two more touchdowns from his high school quarterback, and the Wolverines escaped with a 35-13 victory. The game wasn't on in Chicago, and I can't remember who exactly I was watching, but with every game break or update on ABC, he was scoring again.

Week two was the annual match up with Notre Dame, this time at the Big House. If anyone in the world of College Football hadn't heard about Desmond yet, they were about to. The Wolverines had lost to Notre Dame four times in a row, and Howard and company were ready to right the ship. After a 4 touchdown performance against Boston College, the Irish were determined to stop Desmond Howard. In 1991 that was easier said than done. Michigan even installed a natural grass field prior to the 1991 season, but nothing could slow Howard down.

Michigan built a 17-0 lead, and had to get creative to have the ball in #21 hands. The Wolverines were playing well, and Ricky Powers, then the full time starter with Vaughn in the NFL, had a big game running through huge holes that Michigan's line was creating. Grbac tossed the ball to Powers near the 29 yard line, and he handed it to Howard on the end around. Howard sliced through the Notre Dame defense and found himself in familiar territory, the end zone. On the play, Notre Dame had all but contained the reverse, but a lightning quick cut at full speed was all he needed to move into the secondary and the race was on. Howard crossed the goal line with his left hand raised in celebration with Irish defenders diving behind him. The Wolverines continued to play well, but Notre Dame came storming back. They would close the gap to 17-14 behind the strong play of Rick Mirer.

Late in the 4th quarter, with Michigan nursing a 17-14 lead, Gary Moeller had a decision to make. Michigan faced a 4th and 1 at the Irish 25 yard line. A field goal would put Michigan up 6, and Notre Dame could win with a touchdown. Ricky Powers was having a huge game, and the line was blocking well. If Bo was still in charge, I am positive that Michigan faithful would be talking about Ricky Power's famed two yard plunge to seal the game. Although the final decision maker on that 4th and 1 call is debatable, "Moeller" decided to put it in the air.

I say that because it is rumored to this day that Elvis Grbac and Desmond Howard saw something and audibled, I guess we'll never know. Either way, during one of the most memorable plays in Michigan and College Football history, the high school friends and teammates would connect again. Grbac would take the snap and drop back to pass. He pumped toward the right side for an apparent short pass and quickly reloaded. Desmond, after a momentary hesitation was racing down the sideline, covered by two Notre Dame defensive backs. Grbac placed the ball in the back corner of the end zone, where Desmond dove the last 8' to catch the ball. The announcer was yelling about the diving catch. The announcers started talking about this "Heisman Trophy" candidate, and would be from that day forward.

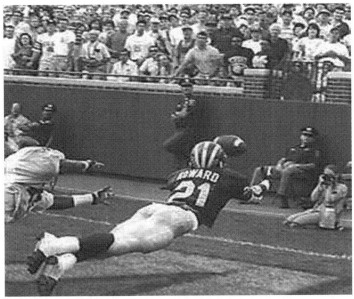

Howard had scored 6 touchdowns through two games, and Desmond Fever was spreading. We were living in Chicago, and the epidemic even reached the western suburbs. High school players from the varsity team down to the freshman "B" team were taping their ankles like #21, and meanwhile Desmond was breaking them week after week. Those taped ankles were often in the highlights, and the fever was spreading. There you go, a uniform trait like Harmon. Two weeks later, after a bye, the schedule brought the Florida State Seminoles to Ann Arbor, led by their

Legendary Coach, Bobby Bowden. Florida State was ranked #1, and Michigan entered the game ranked #3. The media buzzed about the matchups between some of the greatest players in the nation in 1991.

The Seminoles came to town with their own group of heralded players. Their offense was led by Casey Weldon their senior quarterback (2nd in the Heisman Voting in 1991) and the defense was anchored by a shutdown corner Terrell Buckley (8th in the Heisman Voting in 1991). Michigan was riding the momentum of the big win over Notre Dame, and on September 28th 1991, the fireworks started early.

Michigan received the ball first, and Bowden followed the rule and kicked the ball away from Howard. On that first drive, Grbac dropped back and tried to throw a quick hitter to Desmond and Buckley stepped in front of him, intercepted the pass and took it 40 yards for the early 7-0 lead. Ouch. The Wolverines battled back, and on their second possession, Moeller spread the ball around. During the drive, Michigan stayed balanced. Ricky Powers and the offensive line controlled the ball. Grbac finally found Howard on an out pattern. It seemed like the ball hung in the air FOREVER after the first drive, but Grbac got it to his guy. It wasn't a big gainer, but it had to feel good for Grbac and Howard to complete a pass without a speedy Seminole getting their hands on it. The drive would end with a 13 yard corner route from Grbac to Howard, with another acrobatic catch. It was the same corner where they burned Notre Dame two weeks earlier.

Oh that Bobby Bowden. On the next drive Florida State would score on a fake field goal. The fake field goal was set up by a play that will forever stick in my mind. Casey Weldon threw a quick screen to none other than Charlie Ward (1993 Heisman Trophy Winner) the Seminoles backup quarterback who snuck in as a wide receiver. Ward threw the ball back to Weldon who raced down the sideline with most of the offensive line leading the way. Daggumet Coach Bowden. Those Seminole teams were amazing. Michigan's JD Carlson converted on a field goal, and Florida State responded once again. Amp Lee, the FSU tailback raced 44 yards for a touchdown, weaving through the Michigan defense. The ensuing drive ended with a Michigan punt, which Terrell Buckley returned for 30 yards. The Seminoles would score again on a touchdown pass from Weldon to the tight end Leon Hart, and Florida State led 25-10. They had missed an extra point earlier, and attempted a two point conversion that failed. Michigan got the ball back in need of a score.

FSU again kicked away from Howard, but the Wolverines had the ball. As the ABC commentators talked about Michigan needing to play their game, Gary Moeller showed a little bit of Bowden. After a 1st down catch by Yale Van Dyne, Michigan got fancy. From the FSU 42 yard line,

Michigan faked a reverse to Yale Van Dyne. Grbac threw
the ball deep to #21, who was faking in and out on All
American Terrell Buckley. Buckley played Howard
perfectly, but as the ball arrived Desmond was able to make
a spectacular mostly one handed catch. His teammates raced
to the end zone where a smiling Howard had done it again.
The score was 25-17 Florida State. The Michigan comeback
would continue briefly. Michigan linebacker Steve Morrison
would intercept Casey Weldon, Weldon's first interception
of 1991, and returned it deep into Florida State territory.
Elvis Grbac hit fullback Burnie Leggette on a 7 yard
touchdown to bring the score to 25-23. Michigan went for 2,
and Grbac threw a wide receiver screen to Desmond. A
defender disrupted the throw and it fell short. Howard still
caught the ball and moved across the field only to be stopped
at the 1 yard line. I know it's not typical to write about
failed two point conversions, but Howard even made that
attempt exciting…. Look at the tape.

Before the half, Florida State would score again.
Most of the drive came on a long pass from Weldon to Amp
Lee, and on the next play, Lee danced into the end zone on a
sweep with an amazing cutback that caused Michigan
defensive back Lance Dotten to lose his footing. Florida
State would miss another extra point, wide right (☺), don't
worry, not going there, this story is about Michigan. In the
end it wouldn't cost them much.

The fireworks weren't over quite over. Florida State kicked off and Howard nearly made them pay. For one second, the confident Bowden elected to kick off to Desmond, and he caught the ball at the 12 yard line and took off. He returned the ball to the FSU 40 yard line, and would likely have scored if he cut to the left. With 11 Seminoles chasing him, there was Buckley, on special teams, and the showdown continued. Like the 2 point conversion against Michigan State in 1990, I bet Howard would love another chance to cut one more time. Michigan drove the ball and had a first and goal at the 4 yard line. On a 3rd and goal, Michigan attempted to use Howard as a decoy, and Grbac threw back across the field to tight end Tony McGee. The pass was intercepted. The score at halftime was 31-23 in one of the most memorable halfs in Michigan Football history. It was the most points ever scored in a half at Michigan Stadium. Desmond had 128 all-purpose yards.

During the halftime show Bo Schembechler of all people was performing analysis for ABC Sports. Bo stated the defense that responded would determine the outcome of the game, and additionally that it was concerning for Michigan that they could not control the ball and move it on the ground. In the end, Schembechler was right as usual. The Seminoles were #1 for a reason however, and Michigan would fall 51-31. Although the Wolverines lost, they didn't go down easy, and Desmond Howard proved that he could perform against the best teams in the nation. I don't know if there has ever been more talent on the field in Ann Arbor at one time with Heisman Trophy candidates and NFL picks galore.

Despite the setback and the implications on Michigan's championship hopes, the 1991 season would still be one to remember. Michigan won the rest of their regular season games and the Big Ten Championship. They beat Iowa 43-24, and Howard accounted for two more touchdowns. The next week was a revenge game against Michigan State after the events of 1990. Michigan blasted the Spartans on the road 45-28. Howard scored two more touchdowns, during a 108 yard receiving day. They beat Indiana 24-16, and Howard was held to five catches, and only 36 yards. Three of those catches however, went for touchdowns. Desmond would also rack up 109 yards in kickoff returns, 71 on one return. The Hoosier's had their own Heisman candidate that day, running back Vaughn Dunbar (6th in the Heisman Voting in 1991) but Howard stole the show.

The week after the Wolverines dominated Minnesota in the Metrodome. At that point, you would think that Minnesota would have a plan to slow down Howard, but it didn't matter. 155 yards receiving and two more touchdowns later, the Wolverines had dominated the Gophers 52-6. Purdue came to the Big House, assumedly with a plan to slow down #21. They left with a 42-0 loss, and got to watch Desmond celebrate in the end zone with his teammates two more times. The Northwestern Wildcats also came to the Big House and were dominated 59-14. Thinking about the season remaining and doing what MICHIGAN coaches do, Moeller held Howard out of much of the second half. He still caught 4 passes for 102 yards and a touchdown, but the coach was unloading the bench and enjoying the level that his TEAM was playing at.

Michigan traveled to Champaign Urbana to face Illinois on 11/16/1991, and during the 20-0 victory, Desmond again found the end zone, twice. He caught one and ran for one, and Michigan was 9-1 and ranked #3 once again when the ohio state buckeyes came to the Big House. Magic was about to happen...

On November 23, 1991, Michigan continued their impressive campaign. They took a 7-0 lead on a one yard touchdown run by fullback Burnie Leggette. Although the buckeyes battled and stayed close, lightning was about to strike. Ted Williams, the osu punter launched a punt to Desmond Howard, and the rest is history. I have seen the play so many times that I remember the commentary, the immortal Keith Jackson, the voice of College Football was calling the game. Keith Jackson surely had seen a lot of things throughout his amazing career covering this game. Never however, had he seen anything like what was about to happen. It was something to the effect of **WILLIAMS IN TO PUNT**, something about his average, **NICE HIGH PUNT, GOT A LITTLE WIND UNDER IT, OH MY GOODNESS, LOOK AT THAT, ONE MAN, GOOODBYYEEE, HELLOO HEISMAN**! Howard took the punt back 93 yards from the 7 yard line and the Big House crowd roared. At the end of his race into the end zone, Howard paused briefly and posed with a likeness of the most prestigious individual award in College Football, the Heisman Memorial Trophy.

It was Howard's 23rd touchdown of the year. The Heisman debate of 1991 was resolved during those 93 yards. The Elvis Grbac to Desmond Howard connection tied the record for the most prolific in College Football history at the conclusion of the 1991 season. Although they wouldn't connect on that day, from 1989 to 1991 they connected on

31 touchdown passes. Not bad for two high school teammates from Cleveland, Ohio. Who knew that when a spunky young Howard recruited his quarterback from the basketball team at St. Joseph's high school, that the tandem would re-write the record book.

Bo Schembechler was again on the halftime show, providing analysis for ABC Sports in New York. Bo praised the Michigan defense, and chastised the Michigan offense, but oh the smile when he talked about Desmond Howard's 93 yard punt return. The halftime show began with a look back at Bo's first victory over ohio state, and there was nothing more fitting on that day. The guy who came to play for Bo, and who Bo and Gary Moeller moved to WR was on the verge of winning the first Michigan Heisman Trophy since Tom Harmon. Michigan won 31-3.

On December 14th, 1991, at the Downtown Athletic Club in New York City, Desmond Kevin Howard, son of JD and Hattie, was awarded the 1991 Heisman Memorial Trophy. The 5'9" 180 pound lightning rod received 2077 total votes, while Casey Weldon finished 2nd with 503. Fittingly, Howard ran away with award, posting the largest margin in the awards history at the time. His run to the award included head to head matchups with 4 of the other Top Ten Finishers. Those taped ankles were the uniform trait for #21.

1991 HEISMAN TROPHY VOTING RESULTS

PLACE	NAME	SCHOOL	CLASS	POSITION	1	2	3	TOTAL
1	DESMOND HOWARD*	MICHIGAN	JR.	WR	640	68	21	2077
2	CASEY WELDON	FLORIDA STATE	SR.	QB	19	175	96	503
3	TY DETMER	BYU	SR.	QB	19	129	130	445
4	STEVE EMTMAN	WASHINGTON	JR.	DT	29	100	70	357
5	SHANE MATTHEWS	FLORIDA	JR.	QB	11	72	69	246
6	VAUGHN DUNBAR	INDIANA	SR.	TB	6	51	53	173
7	JEFF BLAKE	EAST CAROLINA	SR.	QB	7	29	35	114
8	TERRELL BUCKLEY	FLORIDA STATE	JR.	DB	1	24	51	102
9	MARSHALL FAULK	SDSU	FR.	RB	0	10	32	52
10	BUCKY RICHARDSON	TEXAS A&M	SR.	QB	6	9	9	45

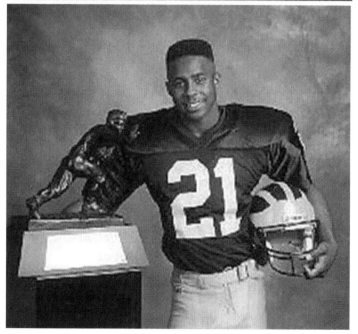

Michigan would go on to face Washington in the Rose Bowl with their National Championship hopes still alive. Washington had the nation's #1 ranked defense and finally came up with a formula to slow down #21. My heart sank as the Wolverines fell 34-14, and Washington players were anything but shy, with several flashing the Heisman Pose throughout the game. Mario Bailey, the Washington WR was one of them, and after the game the usually quiet Howard responded accordingly. In an interview, Howard told reporters that Bailey was welcome to come to his house to look at the real thing, referring to the Heisman Trophy. Despite the loss to Washington, 1991 was one of the greatest and most memorable in Michigan History. The team was loaded, and Howard's performance elevated the Wolverines to greater heights. Every bit as memorable as each diving touchdown catch was the infectious smile you could see on TV despite the helmet and mouth guard. This Ohio native had the Big House rocking, and after all 23 scores he was mobbed by his teammates. Typically, he would jump into the arms of the closest one that could lift him. If he was quiet or reserved off the field, he sure wasn't on it. Howard put on a display to remember in 1991. This ultimate **MICHIGAN MAN** further defined the evolving definition as well as the *"THREE MICHIGAN HEISMAN CRITERIA"* established by Tom Harmon 51 years earlier. This superstar from enemy territory never lost to ohio state.

DESMOND HOWARD

#21

ATTRIBUTES:

1. INCREDIBLE HANDS
2. BLAZING SPEED
3. GOD GIVEN ABILITY TO MAKE PEOPLE MISS
4. BURNING DESIRE TO SUCCEED

THE STATISTICS

RECEIVING

YEAR	RECEPTIONS	YARDS	AVERAGE	TOUCHDOWNS
1989	9	136	15.1	2
1990	63	1025	16.3	11
1991	62	985	15.9	19
CAREER	134	2145	16	32

RUSHING

YEAR	ATTEMPTS	YARDS	AVERAGE	TOUCHDOWNS
1989	5	11	2.2	0
1990	5	58	11.6	0
1991	13	180	13.8	2
CAREER	23	249	10.8	2

KICK RETURNS

YEAR	RETURNS	YARDS	AVERAGE	TOUCHDOWNS
1989	12	295	22.7	0
1990	17	504	29.6	1
1991	15	412	27.5	1
CAREER	44	1211	27.9	2

PUNT RETURNS

YEAR	RETURNS	YARDS	AVERAGE	TOUCDOWNS
1989	0	0	0	0
1990	6	55	9.2	0
1991	18	282	15.7	1*
CAREER	24	337	14	1

ALL CONFERENCE TEAMMATES:

J.D. Carlson, Dean Dingman, Greg Skrepenak, Erick Anderson, Matt Elliot, Mike Evans, Ricky Powers, Elvis Grbac, Chris Hutchinson

ALL AMERICAN TEAMMATES:

Erik Anderson, Matt Elliot, Greg Skrepenak

INDIVIDUAL AWARDS:

The Heisman Memorial Trophy, The Walter Camp Award, The Maxwell Award, AP Offensive Player of the Year, The Dunlop Pro-Am Athlete of the Year

OTHER NOTABLES:

138 points scored are the most in a season at Michigan
640 1st Place Heisman Votes were the most ever by a Winner
19 consecutive games with a scoring catch
Named the 1st ever MICHIGAN LEGEND

THE MOMENT:

*93 yard punt return against OSU, with a memorable pose...

Despite countless plays and performances that were bigger than life, Howard was considered unique during his time in Ann Arbor. He spent most of his off the field time studying and away from the team. Desmond was never one to follow the crowd. Part of that could have been that he always had to work a little harder to achieve his goals. After JD worked so hard for Desmond to attend a private school, the bus would become young Desmond's main transport to school. Hours each day to better his education, and those experiences and traits were what he took with him to Michigan. He had an interest in civil rights, America's past, and studied it all on his own. He lived off campus so he wouldn't be bothered. He quietly took the College Football world by storm with his play alone. His nick name of "Magic" stuck with him long before he arrived on the Michigan Campus. It actually came from one his basketball coaches back in Cleveland, long before Howard would re-write the Michigan record book with Grbac. Howard was as proud of his accomplishments off the field as he was with what he accomplished on it. He left Michigan to enter the NFL draft, but also received his degree. I'm sure that his parents wouldn't have it any other way.

Howard was selected in the first round of the 1992 NFL draft by the Washington Redskins. The Redskins were coming off a Super Bowl Victory, and selected Howard as the most electric play maker in the draft. The Redskin receivers were aging, and Howard went to DC. My family was still in Chicago at the time, and I recall we were rushing to Church the day Desmond scored his first touchdown. Harbaugh and the Bears were probably on TV. I remember a game break, and another returner catching a punt, throwing the ball across the field to #80 Desmond Howard who raced down the RFK Stadium sideline 55 yards for his first NFL score. His best season for the Redskins came in 1994 when he totaled 40 receptions for 727 yards and five touchdowns.

I attended an FCA (Fellowship of Christian Athletes) Football camp during my time in Chicago. We would go out to Plano Illinois, practice during the day, activities after practice, and time studying the Bible in the evening. There were several outstanding high school players from the area there as the counselors, and even one from the NFL. Kent Graham, the Wheaton North High School star, as well the buckeye quarterback in 1991 who had the *pleasure* of watching Desmond racing down the sideline on the famed 93 yard punt return followed by a certain celebration. I wore a Michigan Football shirt to practice one day, and Mr. Graham had a comment. I asked him something about whether he can look back and admit it was one of the greatest moments in College Football history, his reply? "Just needed ketchup and mustard." He didn't think it was funny, but for one brief conversation, I got to back up my **MICHIGAN MAN.**

Even with a productive season in 1994, the Redskins wanted more and made Howard available for the NFL Expansion Draft. As my favorite player struggled, my family was on the move. Moving during your high school career is not an event you look forward to, but it was also part of being an Army brat. I was playing JV football, at safety and running back. I played mostly defense, and had carried the ball less than 20 times during the season. During my last game, we were winning big and I was playing right halfback. We were at the West Chicago 5 yard line, and the call was a 23 blast. "Another touchdown for Billy, oh great" I thought. Our quarterback who I had been in school with since the 6th grade had a Grbac moment. He smiled at me and said to the huddle, "24 blast on two, 24 blast on two, break." I had a big old Desmond grin that my Dad could probably see from the stands. Into the end zone I dove with a smile you could see through a mouth guard. I think Desmond, Elvis, and Coach Moeller would have been proud.

Desmond Howard headed to the Jacksonville Jaguars. He was offered a one year deal by the expansion Jacksonville Jaguars. I would check the stats each week, look for highlights, and kept tabs on him. I got to Fort Knox High School and played Varsity Football in 2005. It was a totally different brand than I experienced in the very competitive Chicago Suburbs, where rosters were around 80. I got to Fort Knox and learned quickly that most played both ways, and that our running back was amazing. So there I was, finally playing varsity football. Friday's were simple for me. Go to school, come home for a quick meal, and oh yeah, my video tapes. There were three things that I watched before every game at Fort Knox High School.

The first was the last fight in Rocky IV. I didn't know any other way to get ready for war than to watch Rocky knock out the invincible Russian killing machine Ivan Drago. The second was the last scene of Top Gun (who never wanted to be Maverick or Goose? That is what I thought). The third clip I would watch was only as long as it took for Michigan's #21 to rip down the East sideline against the buckeyes and strike the famous pose. I was ready. I'd get in the car with my best friend Gene, and we were off. Although I was 5'9" I will admit I was anything but Desmond. I played fullback at 150 pounds because I wasn't afraid to hit, and I was the strong safety. My other assignment however, is what I had been waiting for all those years. I returned punts. Coach Burnett was concerned about our All-State tailback, Derrick Homer, getting too fatigued. As the new kid in town, I got a shot. Burnett loaded up the jugs machine, and I started catching the punts he would launch to me. So that was it, in 1995, I was returning punts. I probably watched a little too much Desmond video over the years, but I knew I could do it. With Homer being the amazing player he was, I knew my moments would come on special teams. Out-kicked me? I'm returning it. Off the bounce? I'm returning it. Inside the 10? Here we go. It worked out for me, I took some back for touchdowns my junior year. I even have most of the video to prove it. You see, Fathers get pretty excited when their sons break loose, and so a typical clip was me catching the ball, finding blockers, and then the camera would find the people next to him, the bleachers, or the autumn sky as my Dad cheered! I was enjoying every minute, and smiling like a certain Heisman Trophy Winner. Desmond Fever was still uncured in Fort Knox, Kentucky. As I said, that's what parents do, from Heisman Trophy winner's parents to the rest of us.

Meanwhile, hampered by an ankle injury and a concussion Desmond's career continued through a rough spot with only 26 receptions and 1 touchdown for the Jaguars in 1995. More surprisingly, he only had 10 kick returns.

My days attempting to imitate Desmond were short lived, as my Father was being transferred again, this time to St. Louis, MO. I was planning to live with a family friend to finish my Football career. It turned out God had other plans. I think he knew that the Gallaghers stick together through it all, and I was injured during a two a day practice in 1996. I got hit while returning a punt, and I mean hard. I have to give it to Torre Mallard. He didn't make a hit like that at any time in 1995. My jaw was broken, and with the thing wired shut, senior year or not, my parents said I was moving. So there I am, living in St. Louis, I didn't know a soul, and my freshman little brother Matt and I were starting a new high school in St. Louis. My favorite player wasn't currently on an NFL roster, and needless to say, I was an angry little man who could only drink Ensure and soup. Ugggh. So there we are, on the verge of school, and I read in one of my 3 preseason football magazines (Big Ten, National College Football, and NFL) that Desmond Howard was in camp with the Green Bay Packers. There was a game that was going to be on TV. On August 12th, 2006, despite being the angriest senior to be in Olivette, MO, I was going to get to watch Desmond. As the game went on, the announcers were talking about the cuts and roster spots. Of course they mentioned his amazing days at Michigan, but they also talked about the career that hadn't panned out. I started thinking, "man, maybe this game is NOT what I need to be watching." I was down, I have to admit, and my favorite player was about to get cut.

You know how it is in the NFL, Wide Receivers wore 80-89, and there was Desmond, rocking #22. Not the best sign for someone destined to be on the final roster of the Green Bay Packers. I was in need of something positive, I cannot lie. I know Desmond was feeling far more pressure than me, but as a fan I was riding it with him. Then, in the third quarter, the Steelers punted, ignoring the rule that applied in 1991 (you didn't kick to Desmond), and it fell in the hands of Desmond Kevin Howard. He caught the punt, made a move, and raced 77 yards for a touchdown. It was an NFL preseason game, I got it. It was a play to secure a roster spot, I got it. To me however, it was a moment to reflect that everything was going to be okay. I celebrated, as much as a guy with a jaw wired shut can, I celebrated. It was like Michigan had just beaten ohio state all over again. Howard made the Green Bay Packers and specialized as a punt and kick returner. He wasn't offered the kind of money he thought he should be making, but Howard seized the opportunity. Against Detroit, late in the 1996-1997 season, Desmond scored on a 92 yard punt return, and again struck that famous pose. Lions fan or not, I celebrated. He ended up being a key player for the Packers, and was constantly putting the Packers in good field position on his signature returns wearing #81. Green Bay made the playoffs led by Brett Favre. In a playoff game against the San Francisco 49ers, Desmond re-introduced himself to America. For those who hadn't heard that Desmond was back outside of Green Bay, they were about to. Howard's 71 yard punt return touchdown gave Green Bay the early 7-0 lead. Later in the game, only a few series later, Desmond returned another punt 40 yards to the 49ers 7. Green Bay rode the quick start to a 35-14 victory.

Another factor in the outcome was that Steve Young, the starting quarterback for the 49ers aggravated a rib injury and had to be relieved by none other than Elvis Grbac. That's right, Howard's high school teammate and the guy that threw him all those touchdowns at Michigan. Although I'm sure Elvis would have preferred a 49er victory, I'm also sure he was pleased to see that the guy who recruited him to play football back in Cleveland on the basketball court had found that electric smile. In the NFC Championship, the Packers faced more **MICHIGAN MEN**, Biakabutuka, Greg Skrepenek, and Matt Elliot. What an amazing sport this is.

The Packers played in Super Bowl XXXI and faced the New England Patriots. He had always performed his best in the biggest games at Michigan, and that Super Sunday in New Orleans would be no different. He tied the Super Bowl record for total yards in a game (244), and scored on a 99 yard kickoff return. Howard later admitted in the New York Times that he was motivated even further for the Super Bowl by the pregame trash talking of Corwin Brown that even spoke about the pose. Brown was a safety on the 1991 Michigan Wolverines Football team. Also on that Patriots team was cornerback Ty Law.

Howard got the last laugh. The performance put him in elite company once again. Howard was named Super Bowl MVP, only the fourth in history at the time to win the

Heisman Trophy and the Super Bowl MVP award. Also on the list are the legendary quarterback Roger Staubach for Navy and then the Cowboys, quarterback Jim Plunkett at Stanford, then the Oakland Raiders, and finally Marcus Allen the great USC running back who played for the Raiders and Chiefs in the NFL.

Desmond Kevin Howard was back in the lime light, and about to land a big free agent deal. For the season, Howard led the NFL in punt returns, punt return yards, and had 3 punt return touchdowns. He also had 460 yards on kick returns and caught 13 passes for 95 yards. His 875 punt return yards were an NFL record.

Things turned out okay for me in St. Louis. The year that started with my freshman brother Matt and I eating together in the cafeteria every day because we didn't know a soul, would end with us both being happy through the magic of sports. I tried out for basketball despite not playing since my freshman year. Although I wavered from 11th to 12th and back to 11th in the lineup, I sure could hit the occasional crowd pleasing three. I met some great friends along the way. My little brother played soccer and was the only kid in the history of Ladue High School that could execute the front flip throw in. After one more Gallagher move to Pennsylvania for a brief assignment, my brother would graduate from that same school. So as I watched Desmond win the Super Bowl MVP award that winter, all was good.

Following one of the greatest performances in Super Bowl history, Howard signed with the Oakland Raiders for a reported 4 years and 6 million dollars. Howard made closer to the NFL minimum in Green Bay around $300,000 per year. In his first season in Oakland, he was able to keep rolling. He led the NFL in kickoff returns and kickoff return yards. He remained with the Raiders through the 1998 season, and went back to Green Bay in 1999. Before going back to Green Bay however, let me point out that one of his teammates was CHARLES WOODSON. More on him later, but Oakland had two Michigan Heisman winners. Following the 1999 NFL season, the Packers released Desmond Howard and it looked like a great career at that point might be coming to an end. It turned out that "Magic" had a little more to prove, and of all places he would do it in Detroit with the Lions. He signed with the Lions four days after the Packers let him go, late in 1999. In his first game for Detroit, the Lions would ride a 68 yard Desmond Howard punt return touchdown to a 33-17 win over Washington. In the opener of the 2000 season, a 14-10 victory at New Orleans, he struck again with a 95yard touchdown return. That is right, the same venue where Howard earned the Super Bowl MVP award in provided another signature moment. Although that score was the only touchdown on the season for Desmond Howard, his efforts would lead him to his first and only Pro Bowl following the season. Selected as the NFC's kick returner, there was a familiar face selected to play quarterback for the AFC. It was Elvis Grbac. Each had journeyman careers in the NFL. I find it amazing that they were each selected for the Pro Bowl only once, and that was following the 2000 season. Nine years after THE CATCH and THE POSE, and 13 since the two left Ohio to play for the enemy. An even better twist in the story is who was coaching the Lions during that season. Bobby Ross was at the beginning of the season, but resigned after nine games. The interim Head Coach? GARY MOELLER, Desmond's coach at Michigan. I can't make this stuff up people, but what a story.

It all seemed fitting for Howard and Grbac and you have to think the bond was strong. Although that is a view from outsider, a fan that followed the two's careers on TV and through the media, the suspected bond is one that I can certainly relate too. For me, it was formed through a journey that started at Xavier University in 1997. I met Sean, another sports fan, who would quickly become my best friend. We roomed together our last three years in College, both on scholarship through Army ROTC. We left Xavier in 2001 and could be stationed anywhere based on the needs of the Army. Sure, you make requests, but I never would of thought we would both be on our way to the 82nd Airborne Division, or even part of the same combat Brigade. We were. We even jumped out of planes together.

In 2002, we found ourselves on an aircraft heading to Kuwait, and even sat together on that plane. After 4 years talking football, drinking beer, chasing girls, and studying (yes that is the correct order Mom and Dad) we found ourselves in a strange place. We were leading soldiers in the United States Army. We sat in the same mission briefs, and occasionally Sean's guys even provided the armed escort for my unit's travels. During that same deployment to Operation Iraqi Freedom, we were to conduct a RIP/TOA (Relieve In Place/Transfer Of Authority) meeting for a sector of Baghdad with a unit from the 101st Airborne Division.

My teammate and best friend from Fort Knox High School was Gene. He was the guy who would watch Desmond and Rocky with me pregame and played football at Army as a defensive tackle. I knew he was in the 101st Airborne. That's all I knew. There were around 15,000 people in each of our combat teams, and there are more than a million soldiers in the United States Army if you count Active Duty, the Reserves, and the National Guard. My odds of seeing these two individuals were probably still better than the 1/10,240 odds of winning the Heisman based on MY God given talent, but I cherish the moments to this day.

On a hot and sandy afternoon at a water treatment plant in Baghdad, in walked Genezo. I was shocked, and spurted a Coach Burnett Fort Knox Football quote. After a rough preseason scrimmage in Kentucky during 1995 against Meade County, the coach was hot. It went something to the effect of *"You embarrassed yourselves, your coaches, your school, Fort Knox Kentucky, and the da*% UNITED STATES OF AMERICA…go to church Sunday, and be here for practice by 2pm, tell your preacher to pray for your @%.."* The lines stopped another young patriot dead in his tracks and he knew who it was. There are only around 40 people in the world privileged enough for that deserved butt chewing by Coach Burnett. There are some kids in Pelham, Alabama right now who may have heard something similar. The laughter and noise surely raised eyebrows for the rest of the soldiers in the water treatment plant, but hey, what could we do? In our 15 minutes together we even discussed the upcoming Big Ten season, Gene is big Penn State fan. We all got home safe, and if I could only count the times Sean would remind me of the "CO" before Michigan's 1997 Championship, I would have another great statistic for this book. Back to the story and Michigan's #21.

Howard ended his NFL career after the 2002 season and retired after being cut by Detroit. Howard is still a major figure in and out of football, and currently works for ESPN as an analyst and key figure on the popular program ESPN College Game day. He travels the country with the program to most of the marquee games throughout the

College Football season. His contagious smile and passion for the game come out during every program. My amazement sometimes is how he remains objective when discussing Michigan, but that is Howard, a true professional. In May of 2010, Desmond Kevin Howard was inducted into the College Football Hall of Fame. As an analyst, Howard isn't afraid to speak his mind. Outside of his ESPN career, Howard remains involved with the University of Michigan. He appears at Alumni events and Charity Basketball games. He provides motivational speaking services for various events and organizations. Desmond Howard makes himself available for speaking events through his website, while traveling across the nation covering College Football. Even more recently, Howard became the first Michigan player to be named a *MICHIGAN LEGEND*, a new tradition set in place to honor players without actually retiring a jersey. There is a patch on the #21 jersey honoring Desmond as a Legend. During the Michigan vs Notre Dame in 2011, Michigan's first ever home night game, there was an emotional Howard in front of the Big House crowd. When I first started this project, I had a goal of convincing #21 to write a forward. In September 2011, as it turned out Howard released his own book. It's great and I assure you this was well underway when I saw it. Thanks for the memories Desmond, and maybe I will meet you on the next one.

1993-1995

THOSE WHO CAME CLOSE

1993, TYRONE WHEATLEY # 6

Tyrone Wheatley was a football and track star before arriving at Michigan, showcasing his skills in Detroit. He came from a mostly broken home, but overcame it all to become one of the most accomplished 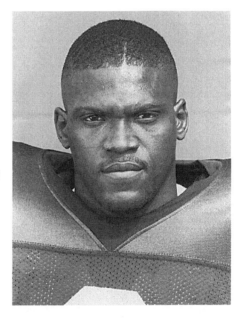 athletes in Michigan high school history. He played at Robichaud High School where he dominated in football as well as track and field. He was a state champion 9 different times between track and field and football. Some were individual championships, and two were for team events (football and track& field). This athlete born in Dearborn, Michigan played eight different high school football positions and was Mr. Football in the State. Wheatley arrived at Michigan with credentials.

He was a freshman in 1991 and spent most of his freshman year as Ricky Powers' understudy and special teams. He was sometimes found with Desmond Howard deep as the other kick returner and lead blocker. As accomplished an athlete as Wheatley was in high school, he got a stern challenge early in his Michigan career. As a freshman, Wheatley ran for 548 yards and NINE touchdowns. Bo Schembechler challenged Wheatley to decide if he was a track man that played football, or a football player that ran track. Oh to be challenged by BO! Wheatley responded. In 1992, Tyrone Wheatley had gained weight, developed a more physical running style, and put on a show in the Big Ten which garnered him the Offensive Player of the Year Award. He opened the season with a touchdown in a tie with Notre Dame. Notre Dame was led by Heisman Trophy candidate running back Reggie Brooks (5th in Heisman voting in 1992.) Against Houston, he exploded for 99 yard kickoff return touchdown. Rushing at Iowa in 1992, Wheatley would arrive. He ran for 226 yards on 19 carries and scored 3 touchdowns. The following week he would lead Michigan to a 35-10 victory over the rival Spartans, accounting for 173 yards on 28 carries and two more touchdowns.

Wheatley continued to impress through the Big Ten schedule and in the season finale against ohio state on the road, Wheatley would run for 110 yards on 19 carries. The game would end in a 13-13 tie. Michigan would win the Big Ten Title at 8-0-3, and go to Pasadena once again to face Washington in the Rose Bowl.

For me, and a million other Michigan fans it was a game about redemption and revenge. More than anything, I couldn't take any more Huskies copying Desmond's pose, or running their mouths. Michigan was talented once again, and 3 TIES away from a much larger picture. I was hopeful. They had a strong defense. Tyrone Wheatley was a FOOTBALL player, and Elvis was still under center. The VCR was rolling.

~~MTV VIDEOS+SHOWS~~ 1993 ROSE BOWL-DON'T TOUCH, MANAGEMENT

Washington returned with a dynamic, but different team. During the 1992 Rose Bowl against the Wolverines, Billy Joe Hobert was the quarterback for Washington. He became the starter after a Mark Brunell knee injury. After an NCAA investigation into Hobert receiving a loan that he would repay after "he made his NFL money," he was no longer a quarterback at Washington, and Brunell was back. So there they were, undefeated with 3 ties, back in the Rose Bowl where things didn't go well in 1992.

The 1993 Rose Bowl would be a classic battle. Washington struck first but Michigan led 10-7 in the first quarter before Elvis Grbac found tight end Tony McGee on a 51 yard touchdown. Then Wheatley broke loose for his first touchdown, on a day that would become one of the greatest Bowl performances in Michigan History. On a trap play in the 2nd quarter Wheatley exploded on a 3rd and 7. With Doug Skene leading the way, he would go untouched for a 56 yard touchdown. Former Washington cornerback Dana Hall was interviewed in the first half. Hall was the cornerback assigned to Desmond in the 1991 Rose Bowl, at the time playing in the NFL. Hall talked about the game, as well as the year before claiming Desmond didn't respect him, and that they handled the tough assignment. My blood as a fan was boiling. I remember commenting to my Dad that no matter what happened, it looked like Michigan was there to play.

Mark Brunell and the Huskies came back firing. After back to back touchdown passes of 64 and 18 yards, Michigan trailed 21-17 at halftime. Luckily for the Wolverines, Wheatley would have a big second half as well. The famous rule was in effect, and Washington would not kick to Wheatley, again the ultimate sign of respect. On his first carry of the 2nd half, Wheatley would take off again, this time for 88 yards and a touchdown. Michigan led 24-14. Announcers Dick Vermeil and Brent Musberger provided the explanation as Wheatley exploded. The play started to the left and finished on the right sideline. I believe Vermeil exclaimed "WHOOOO," as he broke into open field. The Huskies would respond and led 31-24 in the third quarter, only to see Tyrone do it again. The score was tied at 31 near the end of the third quarter as Wheatley exploded one more time for 24 yards and his third touchdown. On his way to perhaps the greatest performance in a bowl game in Michigan history, Wheatley would continue to fight back spasms as he did through much of the game. Michigan won on a late touchdown from Elvis Grbac to Tony McGee with 5:29 to go. Washington would challenge, but the Michigan defense held on.

1993 ROSE BOWL

Scoring		Wolverines		Huskies
First Quarter		16	First Downs	19
M	Elezovic, 41-yard field goal	308	Net Yards Rushing	105
WA	Turner, 1-yard run (Hanson kick)	175	Net Yards Passing	308
M	McGee, 49-yard pass from Grbac (Elezovic kick)	66	Total Plays	74
Second Quarter		483	Total Yards	413
M	**Wheatley, 56-yard run (Elezovic kick)**	30/17/0	PA/PC/Int	31/18/0
WA	Shelley, 64-yard pass from Brunell (Hanson kick)	6/37.0	Punts/Avg	5/39.2
WA	Bruener, 18-yard pass from Brunell (Hanson kick)	28	Return Yards	19
		1/0	Fumbles/Lost	1/1
Third Quarter		8/72	Penalties/Yards	5/43
M	**Wheatley, 88-yard run (Elezovic kick)**	28:12	Time of Possession	31:48
WA	Kaufman, 1-yard run (Hanson kick)			
WA	Hanson, 44-yard field goal			
M	**Wheatley, 24-yard run (Elezovic kick)**			
Fourth Quarter				
M	McGee, 15-yard pass from Grbac (Elezovic kick)			

Rushing-- (M): **Wheatley 15-235**; E. Davis 9-35; R. Powers 9-28; Legette 5-12; Grbac 1-(-2) (WA): Kaufman 20-39; Brunell 10-32; Turner 5-18; Thomas 2-8; Jones 2-4; Barry 4-4

Passing-- (M): Grbac 17-30-175 (WA): Brunell 18-30-308; Bjornson 0-1-0

Receiving-- (M): McGee 6-117; Smith 3-19; Alexander 3-18; Hayes 1-10; Malveaux 1-5; Wheatley 2-4; Legette 2-4 (WA): Shelley 3-100; Bruener 4-85; D. Barry 2-61; Mack 2-33; Kralik 2-16; Jones 2-10; Turner 1-4; Kaufman 2-(-1)

MICHIGAN 38 WASHINGTON 31

Michigan prevailed 38-31 in an evenly matched Rose Bowl. I was excited for Michigan, Wheatley, Grbac, and all of us that suffered through the Rose Bowl in 1992. Wheatley rushed for 235 yards on 15 carries (if only no back spasms) and three touchdowns. Michigan finished the season 9-0-3, and Wheatley would be a prime Heisman candidate in 1993.

Michigan opened the 1993 season with a victory over Washington State. Wheatley led the way with 117 yards on 15 carries and 1 touchdown. In week 2 during a loss to Notre Dame, #6 would score twice and run for 146 yards. After the setback, the Wolverines would win two straight against Houston and Iowa, and his dominance would continue. Although Michigan would not accomplish all of their team goals, #6 would have two consecutive 100 yard games before being shut down by Michigan State. The Spartans limited Tyrone to 33 yards on 11 carries in the 17-7 loss. After a win against Penn State, in which Wheatley ran for 192 yards, Michigan would drop two games in a row against Illinois and Wisconsin in close battles. After wins against Purdue and Minnesota it was time for their ultimate rival. Ohio state came to the Big House and the Wolverines were ready. Wheatley ran for 108 yards and the Wolverines won 28-0. In 1993, Wheatley ran for 1,165 yards and scored 13 touchdowns on the ground with another touchdown receiving. The performance led to some Heisman votes.

That "wide receiver" who snuck in against the Wolverines at the Big House in 1991 would be the winner. Florida State's quarterback Charlie Ward dominated with 2,310 total votes.

1993 HEISMAN TROPHY VOTING RESULTS

PLACE	NAME	SCHOOL	CLASS	POSITION	1	2	3	TOTAL
1	CHARLIE WARD	FLORIDA STATE	SR.	QB	740	39	12	2310
2	HEATH SHULER	TENNESSEE	JR.	QB	10	274	110	688
3	DAVID PALMER	ALABAMA	JR.	RB	16	78	88	292
4	MARSHALL FAULK	SDSU	JR.	RB	7	74	81	250
5	GLENN FOLEY	BOSTON COLL.	SR.	QB	5	47	71	180
6	LESHON JOHNSON	N. ILLINOIS	SR.	RB	5	51	59	176
7	J.J. STOKES	UCLA	JR.	WR	3	37	48	131
8	TYRONE WHEATLEY*	MICHIGAN	JR.	RB	2	31	32	100
9	TRENT DILFER	FRESNO STATE	JR.	QB	2	28	29	91
10	ERIC ZEIER	GEORGIA	JR.	QB	0	24	37	85

Wheatley continued to perform at a high level during his time at Michigan. He was on the preseason Heisman watch list in all the annuals, and hoping for Michigan's best season yet in 1994 as a senior. The Wolverines opened the season with victories over Boston College and Notre Dame, but Wheatley was injured. He would return to face the #7 Ranked Colorado Buffaloes led by Heisman Candidates Kordell Stewart and Rashaan Salaam (1994 Heisman Trophy Winner). In one of the most memorable games in the history of Michigan Stadium, Wheatley would be held to 50 yards, but did score a touchdown. Wheatley had just scored a touchdown on a run when Todd Collins hit Tai Streets on a 65 yard touchdown to bring the score to 26-14 Michigan with 3:52 to play. 1994 was looking like another great season at Michigan. Michigan's good fortunes at the Big House on that day would quickly change. Salaam scored on a one yard touchdown to bring Colorado within 5 points at 26-21. Salaam rushed for 141 yards and 2 touchdowns on the day. For the season he would rush for 2,055 yards on his way to the Heisman Memorial Trophy. The Buffaloes attempted an onside kick that Michigan receiver Mercury Hayes (what an awesome name for a wide receiver) was able to easily diffuse. With one first down, Michigan would be ready to run the best play in football depending on who you are cheering for. Running the clock out with the quarterback on their knee, the old victory formation. After two consecutive penalties, Michigan's Tim Biakabutuka would be stopped on a 3 yard gain, and Michigan had to punt. Uh oh I remember thinking. Stewart would find Michael Westbrook for 21 yards that moved the ball to the Colorado 36 yard line. Stewart spiked the ball to stop the clock, and like Michigan fans across the nation and the more than 106,000 people at the Big House, I just needed the game to be over. As Gary Moeller paced the sideline, my Dad and I were pacing the living room. There was 6 seconds remaining in the game. With 3 receivers to the left, and two to the right side, and Michigan's defensive backs about 30 yards deep already, Colorado snapped the ball. Stewart launched a Hail Mary toward the left side of the end zone, with several Michigan defenders in the area as well as Colorado receivers

Rae Carruth and Michael Westbrook. Westbrook caught the ball. Michigan fell 27-26 in one of the most memorable games in College Football history. Oh this game can sometimes break your heart.

Later in 1994, Michigan would run into two more Heisman contenders at the Big House. Undefeated Penn State came to town with a quarterback named Kerry Collins and a tailback named Ki Jana Carter. The two teammates would finish 4th and 2nd in the Heisman voting in 1994. Wheatley and the Wolverines battled. After a first half where # 6 was held to 11 yards on 9 carries, he would again explode. On consecutive 2nd half drives Wheatley would score on 67 and 21 yard runs. Penn State responded and took the lead for good with 2:53 left on a touchdown pass from Kerry Collins to Bobby Engram.

Michigan finished 1994 with an 8-4 record, losing to the buckeyes in Columbus 22-6. They did win the Holiday Bowl 24-14 over Colorado State. Wheatley would close out his Michigan career in that Holiday game with another 84 yards rushing and a touchdown.

There were several injuries throughout his career that prevented him from playing an entire season as the featured back. Wheatley also, like Bell and Lytle, was one of several talented Wolverine backs. During his career he would share time with other memorable backs like Ricky Powers, Jesse Johnson, Ed Davis, and Tshimanga

Biakabutuka. As a senior, Wheatley rushed for 1,144 yards and 12 touchdowns. Wheatley finished his career with 4,178 yards rushing and 47 touchdowns. He also accumulated 6 touchdown receptions and scored on the kickoff return against Houston in 1992. Wheatley didn't place in the Top 10 in 1994, and moved on to the NFL. He is Michigan's fourth all-time leading rusher and also set marks in track and field. His 20 career 100 yard games rank third behind Mike Hart and Anthony Thomas. Wheatley was an All-Big Ten performer in 1992, 1993, and 1994. Reviewing the **"THREE MICHIGAN HEISMAN CRITERIA,"** here are my points on Wheatley. He was a mega recruit, and possibly the most outstanding athlete in the history of Michigan High School Athletics. There was certainly no "Rudy" story for #6. However, Wheatley was from Michigan, and finished 2-1-1 against the buckeyes. During his last battle, Michigan lost to their rival 22-6. Although Wheatley did not win the Heisman Trophy, he will always be remembered as one of the best players ever to wear the maize and blue. He didn't do much juking, and ran as more of a power back, but when you're as fast as Wheatley, you don't need to.

After Michigan, Wheatley would be drafted by the New York Giants, and played 10 years in the NFL. His best NFL season came in 2000, when Wheatley rushed for 1,046 yards and 9 touchdowns for the Oakland Raiders. He played with another Michigan great on that team, Charles Woodson.

The two would be key contributors on a Raiders team that reached the AFC Championship Game. Wheatley fought injuries in the NFL as well, and retired in 2004 following a hamstring injury that he could never completely recover from. With his NFL career behind him, this **MICHIGAN MAN** returned to Ann Arbor with his family to complete his degree in Sports Management. While in school again, Wheatley would be a volunteer track coach for the Wolverines. After receiving his degree, Wheatley returned to where it all started, Robichaud High School. He coached track and then later football. In his first year as the Football coach he took over a 0-9 team. Coach Wheatley would lead his team to 8-1 regular season record, and the school's first playoff appearance in 13 years. After some more stops building his coaching resume, Wheatley became the Running Backs Coach at Eastern Michigan in 2009 under former Michigan Defensive Coordinator and Head Coach Ron English. Tyrone is currently the Running Backs Coach at Syracuse University. Wheatley continues to grow and develop as a coach. If only he could teach his players his amazing God given speed, Mr. Wheatley could simply fly.

1995, TSHIMANGA BIAKABUTUKA, # 21

Tshimanga "Tim" Biakabutuka was a running back at Michigan from 1993-1995. He was born January 24th, 1974 in Kinshasa, Republic of Zaire. During his younger years, Biakabutuka's family moved to Canada and settled in the Montreal area. He started playing Canadian Football in High School and then at CDFEP at Vanier College. Although not one of the more known recruits in the nation, Biakabutuka did enough to catch Michigan's eye, and he was offered a scholarship. He started playing during the 1993 season, and was one of several talented backs on the roster. In a win over Purdue in 1993, Biakabutuka would receive significant playing time and he took advantage of it. Like moments that all of us have throughout our lives, when they come, you have to take advantage. On 24 carries he ran for 140 yards and scored two touchdowns.

In 1994, with Tyrone Wheatley battling injuries and Biakabutuka was establishing himself as a dependable new option for the Wolverines. His carries and yards increased. As Wheatley's backup, Touchdown Tim was hitting his groove. He ran for 783 yards and 7 touchdowns. Biakabutuka had 100 yard games against Boston College (131), Notre Dame (100), Michigan State (141), and Purdue (100). Wheatley departed after a highly successful career, and Tshimanga Biakabutuka was ready to take the starting role in 1995. Also that offseason, Michigan would have a coaching change. Gary Moeller had coached the Wolverines since Bo's retirement. Prior to the 1995 season however,

Moeller resigned his position after an ugly incident at a restaurant in Southfield, Michigan. Moeller was arrested for drunk and disorderly conduct. We all make mistakes, but they certainly get more attention when you are the Head Coach of the Michigan Wolverines.

Lloyd Carr, a long-time Assistant at Michigan, who came to Michigan with Moeller from Illinois was named the Interim Head Coach for 1995.

1995 would be a season during which not only Michigan fans and Big Ten announcers, but the rest of the College Football World would have to get Tshimanga Biakabutuka off their tongues. During the Wheatley years, Michigan had a very stable quarterback situation. Following Elvis Grbac's graduation, Todd Collins took the reins and guided Michigan's offense at a high level. The transition was a smooth one as Collins had played while Grbac was injured. Things were different in 1995 for Lloyd Carr. For the first time since Elvis showed up with Desmond Howard in 1989, Michigan was not sure who the quarterback was. Scott Dreisbach and a guy named Brian Griese, a walk on, were battling for the job. For Carr, there were also plenty of new faces on defense, and he had to come up with a game plan. The offensive line was deep, big, and experienced. In the two deep there were some Michigan greats. Jon Runyan, Jon Jansen, Zach Adami, and Rod Payne among others. In his first season as the Head Coach at the University of Michigan, Lloyd Carr was going to run the football.

In the season opener, Virginia came to town led by the twins' duo of Tiki and Rhonde Barber. Although Biakabutuka and the running game were held in check, Michigan would win the game as time expired on a touchdown pass from Dreisbach to Mercury Hayes. In week two against Illinois, "Touchdown Tim" would score three times and rushed for 97 yards on only 10 carries. Memphis came to the Big House the following week and Biakabutuka rushed for 143 yards and two more touchdowns. For Lloyd Carr, and an inexperienced group of quarterbacks, it was "in Tim and the Line we trust." The following game was at Boston College, and it would be another 129 yards and touchdown for the running back from Montreal. The following week brought Miami (Ohio) and # 21 had another 98 yards and a touchdown while getting some rest.

Against Northwestern the following week in the Big House, the Wolverines would lose their first game of the 1995 season. It certainly wasn't from a lack of effort, but that was a big year for the Wildcats. They were led by their own Heisman candidate, running back Darnell Autry (4th in Heisman Voting in 1995). In a head to head matchup with another great back Biakabutuka shined. He carried the ball 34 times in the game for 213 yards. The next week at Indiana he would have another 100 yard day, 111 to be exact.

On October 28th, 1995, Minnesota came to Big House. Biakabutuka ran for 196 yards on 19 carries and scored twice. Like I said, people outside Michigan and the Big Ten were trying to get the name right. The Wolverines would fall for the 2nd time the following week against the rival Spartans led by quarterback Tony Banks and wide receiver Nigea Carter on offense. Biakabutuka would have another big day in the losing effort (191 yards on 37 carries, 1 touchdown), but the Wolverines fell short. Two weeks later, Michigan lost again, this time at Penn State, despite 139 yards and touchdown from # 21. So there Michigan was 8-3 heading into the annual battle with ohio state.

On November 25th, 1995 Biakabutuka and the Wolverines were in a spoiler's role against their arch rival led by running back and Heisman candidate Eddie George. Ohio state was having a great season and came to Michigan Stadium ranked # 2 in the nation behind only Nebraska. They had Terry Glenn at wide receiver, and Bobby Hoying (#10 in the Heisman Voting in 1995) under center. The hype about the Heisman had the list narrowed down to George, Nebraska quarterback Tommie Fraizer, and Florida quarterback Danny Wuerffel. The buckeyes were 11-0 and eyeing a National Championship. Biakabutuka and the Wolverines didn't believe the hype. In one of the greatest performances in Michigan history, the offensive line would open gaping holes against the # 2 team in the nation, and those holes were all that "Touchdown Tim" needed. Despite entering the game with a leg injury and a sleeve covering his left calf, Biakabutuka was about to put on a show. In the first quarter, the statistics were staggering. Five carries for 104 yards. Usually a statistic like that is comprised of a run of 80 yards, and 4 short ones. On November 25th, that wasn't the case. His runs were more like 18, 30, 24... time after time.

By halftime, he had rolled up nearly 200 yards. Surely John Cooper, the Head Coach at osu and his staff would have a plan to slow down Biakabutuka in the 2nd half, right? Technically, I suppose they did, but when the clock hit 0's at the end of the game, Michigan had defeated their unbeaten rivals 31-23. George did rush for 104 yards on 21 carries, but Biakabutuka would have the 2nd greatest rushing performance in Wolverine history. His 313 yards on 37 carries with a touchdown was one of the greatest performances ever by a Michigan back. Lloyd Carr had the interim lifted from in front of his Head Coach title earlier in the season, but he was able to win his first game against ohio state. George would go on to win the Heisman, but for one day, Biakabutuka was the talk of College Football....

BaxcbatukiA, did you hear about that guy from Michigan? 313 yards against osu? WOW. **MICHIGAN MAN.**

Michigan would go on to play Texas A&M in the Alamo Bowl but fell 22-20. # 21 again surpassed 100 yards rushing on the day but it wasn't enough. Biakabutuka finished the season with 1818 yards rushing and 12 touchdowns, good for 4th in the nation and STILL the Michigan record for rushing yards in a season.

1995 HEISMAN VOTING RESULTS

PLACE	NAME	SCHOOL	CLASS	POSITION	1	2	3	TOTAL
1	EDDIE GEORGE	OHIO STATE	SR.	RB	268	248	160	1460
2	TOMMIE FRAZIER	NEBRASKA	SR.	QB	218	192	158	1196
3	DANNY WUERFFEL	FLORIDA	JR.	QB	185	152	128	987
4	DARNELL AUTRY	NORTHWESTERN	SO.	RB	87	78	118	535
5	TROY DAVIS	IOWA STATE	SO.	RB	41	80	119	402
6	PEYTON MANNING	TENNESSEE	SO.	QB	10	21	37	109
7	KEYSHAWN JOHNSON	USC	SR.	WR	9	10	12	59
8	TIM BIAKABUTUKA*	MICHIGAN	JR.	RB	1	11	6	31
9	WARRICK DUNN	FLORIDA STATE	JR.	RB	2	3	17	29
10	BOBBY HOYING	OHIO STATE	SR.	QB	0	9	10	28

Looking back at the *"THREE MICHIGAN HEISMAN CRITERIA,"* Biakabutuka was an absolute diamond in the rough for the Wolverines, although not a super recruit. He also wasn't really from enemy territory, unless you consider our neighbor nation to the North a threat. Despite missing on the first 2, there is no denying that he brought it home against the buckeyes in the season finale.

He left Michigan with 2810 yards rushing and 24 touchdowns, and was drafted by the Carolina Panthers. He would spend 6 seasons in the NFL where he was able to achieve 3319 total yards and scored 17 career touchdowns. He too got a close up view of the Desmond show for the Packers in 1996. After football, Biakabutuka entered the restaurant business and now currently owns restaurants in the Southeast. You can find this **MICHIGAN MAN** back in Ann Arbor from time to time, at alumni and charity events, giving back to the school and community where he grew from unknown to unstoppable against the buckeyes.

<u>CHARLES WOODSON</u>
<u>LIGHTNING STRIKES TWICE</u>

Charles C. Woodson was born October 7th, 1976 in Fremont Ohio. Fremont, Ohio is 90 miles from Michigan Stadium, and 104 miles from ohio stadium. Fremont is a working class, Midwestern town. He grew up there and would eventually attend Ross High School. The same Ross High School that Rob Lytle attended. Woodson was an accomplished athlete. As a running back, he would rush for 3,861 yards. During his senior year, the total was 2,028 yards rushing, while also playing defensive back. The performance was good enough for Mr. Football in the State of Ohio, and a young Charles Woodson had options regarding College Football. He was also selected for the USA Today High School All-American Team, and was a Parade High School All-American.

In addition to football, you could find Charles Woodson playing basketball and running track. With many options on where to play to include ohio state, Woodson's older brother had always dreamed of playing for the Wolverines. So as little brothers do, Charles would also be a Michigan fan. When it came time to make a decision, he chose Michigan. It may have been a surprise to fans and recruiters from "the" ohio state university, but there was no surprise within the family. The lines were drawn again in the recruiting wars. Jim Hermann, Michigan's defensive coordinator at the time was a great recruiter. I had the good fortune of meeting Coach Hermann in 1995 at Fort Knox

High School. He was there to recruit Derrick Homer, Kentucky's Mr. Football in 1996, and took a moment to speak with me because Coach Burnett had told him "that boy is a Michigan Fan." We spoke briefly, but it was yet another moment when I got to be a Michigan Man. He was motivating, and gave me some tips on some things he had seen from the tapes while he was watching Homer. Michigan passed on Homer, but he landed his greatest recruit in one Charles C. Woodson the year before. Although Hermann and Head Coach Lloyd Carr recruited Woodson as a defensive back, most schools were recruiting him as a running back. Why wouldn't they? Woodson would make Hermann the happiest coach in America when he accepted Michigan's offer. Not only was Ohio's Mr. Football at running back coming to Michigan, but he wanted to play defensive back. He didn't think he was big enough to survive the weekly pounding as a running back in the Big Ten, so unlike Desmond he had his mind made up before he even arrived on campus. The recruiting strategy paid off, and the superstar from enemy territory was on his way to Ann Arbor.

He got to Michigan in the fall of 1995. Woodson was confident and competitive from the day he arrived. He would compete in that first fall camp, and the coaches were noticing. How good is this freshman with the high white socks? Oh yes, the trait. In Lloyd Carr's first game as the

Head Coach, that miracle win against Virginia on the Mercury Hayes touchdown as time expired, Charles Woodson was on the field. It was 90 degrees in Ann Arbor that day, and everyone needed rest. So Woodson would spell others. The funny thing was however, once he took the field, they couldn't get the freshman off of it. By week two Woodson was starting, and he would start the next 34 in a row. He was out there performing on competitiveness and athletic ability while still learning the schemes and calls. It didn't matter. Week after week, Woodson came through and seemed to get better on every play.

Michigan played Memphis in Ann Arbor, and he made his first collegiate interception. He'd also intercept passes during his freshman season against Minnesota and Purdue. As previously outlined in the Biakabutuka section, ohio state came to the Big House ranked # 2 in 1995, led by their Heisman Trophy Candidate Eddie George, and an All-Big Ten Receiver, Terry Glenn. Glenn had already informed the media that "Michigan was nobody" earlier in the week. Woodson was a competitor, and certainly didn't need anything additional from the mouthy Glenn. While Biakabutuka was running through El Camino sized holes, Woodson and the defense were battling as well. Osu attempted to pick on the freshman cornerback in the first half, and it was working.

Woodson responded. In the 2nd half, # 2 would intercept a buckeye pass that would lead to a Michigan touchdown on a Brian Griese sneak. Osu responded and pulled within 31-23, but there was that man again. Woodson would intercept his 2nd pass, this time to end the game. The freshman from Fremont, Ohio was a buckeye killer. Woodson would be named the Big Ten Freshman of the Year in 1995, as well as All-Big Ten.

In 1996, sophomore Charles Woodson would make even more of an impact. During the offseason, Coach Lloyd Carr approached him about playing some running back in 1996. Woodson suggested receiver and the two had a deal. In 1996, the rest of the Big Ten would have to account for the former Mr. Football on both sides of the ball. Michigan was hoping for a big year, and started the season ranked #11 in the country. They opened the season against Illinois, and a more experienced Woodson would record ten tackles in the Michigan victory. The next week took the Wolverines to Boulder, CO, to battle the Colorado Buffaloes. Michigan would prevail, and Woodson would record his first interception of 1996. He even ran a reverse on that day in Boulder, but it only netted 5 yards. After the 1994 Hail Mary play thrown by Kordell Stewart to Westbrook in the Big House, the 1996 game was set up for another one. It wasn't as far, but as I watched, along with every other Michigan fan, HERE WE GO AGAIN raced through my mind. We were safe, Charles Woodson and Chuck Winters knocked down the pass and Michigan left with a victory. Wheeeew. The Wolverines moved on.

In week four Michigan played UCLA. Woodson would shine during a Wolverine blow out. The final score was 38-9, and # 2 recorded 2 interceptions. Woodson also caught a 13 yard pass as he continued to refresh his offensive skills. Michigan started 1996 4-0, and traveled to play Northwestern. Michigan would drop a heartbreaker due to a late Northwestern comeback. Michigan led 16-0 at the end of the third quarter. The Wildcats clawed back, and won on a late field that would need to be made twice as the whistle blew the first attempt dead. Following the loss to Northwestern, Woodson and the Wolverines would beat Indiana, Minnesota, and Michigan State over the next 3 weeks. Woodson continued to make his mark. Lloyd Carr and his staff continued to find ways to get Woodson the ball.

Against the Spartans on October 26th, they did just that. During the Wolverines 45-29 victory in Ann Arbor he was all over the field. 11 yards on a carry, 6 tackles, 1 interception, and his first trip to the end zone at Michigan. Woodson would catch 2 passes for 28 yards against their in-state rival, and 1 was for a touchdown in the first half. Michigan led 28-10 and didn't look back.

The next week Michigan faced Purdue in West Lafayette, Indiana. Michigan would suffer another disappointing loss. Woodson caught 3 more passes for 43 yards, but as a team Michigan's offense would struggle. Michigan fell 9-3, and didn't find the end zone against the unranked Boilermakers. Purdue Coach Jim Colletto resigned the week prior, effective at season's end. Uggh, I guess that's why they play the game. Michigan fell to # 16 in the Coaches' Poll. Penn State came to Ann Arbor the next week, and the game would end in another Michigan disappointment. Michigan managed to turn the ball over 5 times. Woodson would record 11 tackles, but that usually isn't a good thing if your cornerback has to be that involved. He also broke up a pass on the day. Michigan tried anything to spark the offense, and # 2 returned 3 punts, but it didn't work. The Wolverines fell 29-17 and were struggling heading into their matchup with the # 2 ranked buckeyes. The Wolverines were 7-3, and like 1995, looking for some pride and an upset win over their rival.

Ohio state still had a talented team and even a Heisman candidate in offensive tackle Orlando Pace (4th in the Heisman Voting in 1996). An angry Michigan defense responded by holding the # 2 ranked team in the nation to only 9 points in yet another upset victory. Quarterback Brian Griese, who split time with Scott Dreisbach in 1996, led an improbable Michigan 2nd half comeback in Columbus. That's right, the "walk on" with NFL talent who happened to be the son of the legendary Bob Griese did enough for

Michigan to come out on top. Ohio state led 9-0 at the half, and had missed on several other scoring chances. Griese entered the game after a Dreisbach injury and found Tai Streets for a touchdown on a slant pattern as buckeye All-American cornerback Shawn Springs would slip on the play. Michigan's defense would hold osu to 5 rushing yards and 84 yards total in the 2nd half. Chris Howard, the Michigan running back rushed for 105 yards (84 in the second half) as Michigan held on for the victory. Charles Woodson would break up 2 passes and record 9 tackles on the day. Although the season wasn't going as Michigan expected, they did beat their rival again.

Michigan went to the Outback Bowl to face Alabama. Legendary Coach Gene Stallings was coaching in his last game, and the Wolverines lost 17-14. Michigan led 9-0 and was driving for more points when Brian Griese was hit while attempting a pass. The ball found the hands of Alabama linebacker Dwayne Rudd, who would race 88 yards for the go ahead touchdown. Charles Woodson and the defense did their part, but it wasn't meant to be. Woodson would continue playing everywhere, and even completed a pass for 4 yards. He caught 3 passes for 25 yards, returned 4 punts with a long of 31 yards, and recorded an interception on the day. Despite the disappointing season for Michigan in 1996, Woodson would again be selected for the All-Big Ten team at cornerback, as well as an All-American. For Woodson and the Wolverines however, there were plenty of unanswered questions heading into 1997.

Michigan entered the season ranked #13. They were an experienced team, and mostly in tact from 1996 other than the offensive line. The problem with that is other than the victory over ohio state, 1996 was a disappointment at 8-4. There were winnable games they didn't win. There were turnovers and mental lapses that led to that record. The 1997 roster didn't have a single player who had played in a Rose Bowl, and that hadn't happened since 1969 before Bo Schembechler's arrival. The quarterback controversy of 1996 spilled into the preseason of 1997. Dreisbach, Griese, and a sophomore named Tom Brady were all competing for the job. The offensive line had lost two starters to the NFL, center Rod Payne and guard Damon Denson. Michigan had one offensive lineman, Jon Jansen, who had started a game. The receiving corps was in better shape with Tai Streets and Russell Shaw returning and there were some thoughts about continuing to use # 2 on the offensive side of the ball. The running backs were experienced with running back Chris Howard and fullback Chris Floyd both back. Michigan also had both tight ends returning, but they were breaking in a new kicker. Woodson would anchor the defense, and was joined in the defensive backfield by safety Marcus Ray, Tommy Hendricks, and Andre Weathers who had all contributed in 1996. They had two returning linebackers, but first team All-American Jarrett Irons was gone. There was plenty of talent on the defensive line, but William Carr had moved on to the NFL. Michigan had talent, but there was nothing certain for the Wolverines in 1997. Lloyd Carr and his staff would answer one question prior to the opener, Brian Griese would be the starting quarterback.

Everybody knew about Charles Woodson, and the Mark McGwire rule was in full effect regarding # 2. He was no longer a secret on offense, and it was doubtful that many teams were going to try to throw the ball towards Michigan's superstar. During the preseason, as the team came up with goals, Charles Woodson suggested a simple, all-encompassing one, **JUST WIN**. In response to the uncertainty and disappointments from the prior season, Michigan took Woodson's words to heart.

By the time they opened the season against Colorado, Michigan was ranked #14 in the Coaches Poll. That's right, the Hail Mary guys once again. Colorado was ranked #7, and the Wolverines would find out early in 1997 how the season would go. This time, the game would not come down to a Hail Mary. Michigan led 10-0 at the half, and won 27-3. They displayed a dominant defense, and the offense led by Brian Griese was sharp and efficient. Colorado tested Woodson five times, and he intercepted one of them. The defense would intercept Colorado quarterback John Hessler a total of four times. With Michigan leading 7-0, # 2 caught a 29 yard pass from Brian Griese with 6 seconds left in the half to set up a field goal. It was only one victory, but there was something different about this Michigan team, and Charles Woodson's **JUST WIN** was off to a good start.

The second game was against Baylor in Ann Arbor. Baylor took an early 3-0 lead, but they would not score again. Charles Woodson caught a wide receiver screen for ten yards and a touchdown from Brian Griese. Woodson continued to set the tone for Michigan's season. He would have five unassisted tackles, and 3 were behind the line of scrimmage. On an attempted quick hitting pass, Woodson would provide a Sportcenter highlight on a well-timed hit.

Notre Dame was next on the schedule, and although the game was close Michigan prevailed 21-14. Brian Griese, Chris Howard, and Tai Streets would have strong offensive games as the defense made key stops when necessary. Notre Dame stayed away from Woodson for the most part, and Michigan was on to face Indiana and had climbed to # 6 in the Coaches' Poll. The Wolverines would dominate Indiana in Bloomington. After leading 3-0 after the first quarter, Michigan scored 28 points in the second quarter and cruise to a 37-0 victory. Woodson caught one pass for 21 yards, and the offense didn't need any more than that. The little bit that Indiana did test #2, he made them pay with another interception to go along with 3 more tackles. Indiana wasn't a strong team in 1997, but **JUST WIN** they did.

Northwestern came to the Big House on October 11th, and the Wolverines kept rolling. After Northwestern took a 3-0, Michigan would outscore the Wildcats 23-3. Michigan's offense continued its' consistent and effective play, and the defense would force 2 turnovers and continue to dominate. Woodson caught another pass for 30 yards, recorded 5 tackles, and another interception. Why anyone was still throwing anywhere near Mr. Woodson, I will never know.

The following weekend brought a very talented Iowa team to Ann Arbor. Iowa had a Heisman Candidate of their own in wide receiver/kick returner Tim Dwight (7th in the Heisman Voting in 1997). Iowa running back Tavian Banks would score on a 53 yard touchdown in the second quarter. On the last play of the first half, Dwight would return a punt 61 yards for a touchdown to give Iowa a 21-7 halftime lead. Uh oh, here we go again I thought. I was waiting for Coach Carr to execute the Desmond rules for Tim Dwight, it didn't happen and Michigan paid. After tying the score in the 3rd quarter with 3:11 to go, Dwight returned a kickoff 72 yards to setup an Iowa field goal and a 24-21 lead. Michigan responded again, and Griese threw a two yard touchdown pass to tight end Jerame Tuman with 2:55 remaining in the game. Iowa drove into Michigan territory, but Sam Sword secured the victory with a late interception to end that drive. Woodson returned 6 punts in the game for 70 yards and recorded 6 tackles and broke up a pass. Most of the day would be spent shutting down his assignments and chasing Tim Dwight all over the field. Michigan was ranked # 5, and heading to East Lansing to face the Spartans.

After the blow out in 1996, the Spartans were upset minded on October 25, 1997. In some ways however, I wonder if there was a typo in the game plan. Although Woodson would be contained on offense, Michigan State tried to air it out against the Wolverines and it didn't work. Woodson and safety Marcus Ray would intercept 2 passes each, and Michigan would record 6 total interceptions. Woodson's first interception was one of the greatest plays in Michigan history. Being hurried out of the pocket by Michigan defensive end James Hall, MSU quarterback Todd Schultz attempted to launch the ball down the sideline, likely throwing the ball away when # 2 leaped to make a one handed interception with a one footed landing worthy of a 10 in gymnastics. It took the world to include myself, and replay to figure out what exactly had happened. It was amazing. It was also his 14th interception as a Wolverine, 2nd all-time at Michigan. For Michigan fans like me out there, look at the tape. I still scratch my head on how he did it. They would test Woodson again, and the result was the same.

The defensive back from Fremont, Ohio was being talked about in the Heisman conversations.

For the homecoming game, on came Minnesota in the battle for the Little Brown Jug. Michigan would win 24-3, and there was that man again Charles Woodson. By this point I assume the opponents' game plans said something about accounting for # 2 on both sides of the ball, but nobody seemed to be able to execute it. He scored on a 33 yard reverse, caught a pass, returned 3 punts, and recorded 3 solo tackles. Just another day at the office for #2 Chuck Woodson. **JUST WIN**.

By week 9, Michigan was ranked # 4 in the nation and preparing for the biggest challenge to date, at Penn State. Penn State was ranked #3 in the Coaches Poll and had the 8th ranked offense in the country. Their running back Curtis Enis (6th in the Heisman Voting in 1997) was running wild in the Big Ten. Michigan didn't give Penn State or Enis a chance. On the first offensive play for Penn State, Michigan defensive lineman Glen Steele would set the tone with a sack. They took a 10-0 lead on a touchdown run by true freshman running back Anthony Thomas. Later in the quarter, Griese found a wide open Charles Woodson for a 37 yard touchdown. The shocked Nittany Lion crowd at Beaver Stadium wouldn't have much to cheer about November 8th, 1997. Michigan won 34-8. Michigan was ranked # 2 in Coaches Poll, and # 1 in the Associated Press Poll. The performance was dominant and caught the eye of the College Football nation. Up next? The Badgers of Wisconsin.

Michigan went on the road to Camp Randall Stadium where an upset minded crowd of 79,806 would set the Wisconsin attendance record on that day. Wisconsin was ranked # 24 and ready to ruin the Wolverines season.

Michigan took the opening kickoff and drove 80 yards in 13 plays. Chris Howard would score on a 1 yard touchdown, but Charles Woodson and Brian Griese would hook up again to put them in position. Actually, they hooked up twice on the same play. Griese took the snap and launched a screen to Woodson, who then threw it back to Griese. He moved down the right sideline for 28 yards to the Wisconsin 1 yard line. That's right, Mr. Everything now had a pass completion that nearly went for a touchdown in 1997. Michigan led 16-3 at the half. After a Wisconsin 3rd quarter touchdown, Michigan would add a field goal and another Chris Howard touchdown to extend the lead. Wisconsin would score again, but Michigan held on for the victory 26-16. # 2 continued his diverse dominance in the Big Ten. In addition to his pass completion, he had an interception and caught 3 passes for 27 yards.

Ohio state came to the Big House in a reversed role compared to 1995 and 1996. It was Michigan with a perfect record, and eyes on a National Championship. They had the nation's best defense, and that defense was led by that cornerback from Fremont, Ohio, who defected to Ann Arbor 3 years earlier. He was a primarily defensive player and also performed well enough throughout the season to be a Heisman Trophy finalist. Hype wasn't needed for the matchup, but we all got some anyway. Ohio state wide receiver David Boston had plenty to say before the game, and # 2 would respond. Boston informed the media that ohio state was going to win by 2 or 3 touchdowns. He also had some comments about Woodson specifically. The two teams would settle on the field on November 22nd 1997.

Woodson and Boston even exchanged blows on the field after a play where Boston continued to block Woodson after the whistle. Woodson fired back, and thank goodness he did not get penalized or even ejected. After the week's trash talking, a **MICHIGAN MAN** can't take that from a buckeye, can he? Woodson didn't. After the brief altercation, Woodson put his helmet back on and nodded for the world to see. He was again ready to lead the Wolverines and the Big House roared. The two battled on the field throughout the day. The first ten possessions of the game resulted in one fumble by osu, and 9 total punts. Both defenses were hitting, neither willing to give an inch. In the second quarter, Brian Griese dropped back to pass and hit a crossing Charles Woodson for a 37 yard gain. Anthony Thomas would score on the drive for a 7-0 Michigan lead.

Ohio state was then held to a three and out, and Woodson dropped back to receive the punt. Lightning was about to strike twice at Michigan Stadium. A Heisman candidate, the buckeyes, November, and oh that east sideline. Woodson caught the ball at the 22 yard line near the right hash and weaved to the left sideline, the same sideline where

Desmond raced to the Heisman 6 years before. He coasted to his first career punt return touchdown.

It had happened again. An all too familiar moment for the buckeyes, the Big House was in a frenzy. There would be no "Pose" from #2, who nearly collapsed before being tackled by his teammates. Playing both ways can be a little fatiguing, even for an All-American. The extra point would be blocked, but Michigan led 13-0 and the score would remain until halftime. Let me touch briefly on that blocked extra point. This story is also about the **MICHIGAN MAN,** specifically those who have competed for the Heisman. I also said there are hundreds of these men who never did. The blocked extra point was about to be 2 points for the scarlet and gray when reserve linebacker Rob Swett never gave up and made a tackle 80 yards away. Most don't remember that play, but to me it epitomized the 1997 Wolverines, as well as the **MICHIGAN MAN**. Swett was a SENIOR reserve linebacker.

In the third quarter, ohio state was moving the ball with more success. On the opening drive they moved down the field and were at the Michigan 7 yard line. Buckeye quarterback Stanley Jackson would throw to what he thought was a wide open receiver on a slant pattern only to see it land in the hands of # 2 Charles Woodson. He had done it again. Woodson actually baited the receiver as only All-Americans can do. Michigan would get another huge contribution from the defense when they pressured Stanley Jackson into a hurried throw that would be returned by Andre Weathers 43 yards for a touchdown.

Boston scored a touchdown on a 56 yard reception, but in the end Michigan won the war. The Wolverines offense managed only 189 yards (37 on the Woodson reception). It wasn't pretty, but a certain **MICHIGAN MAN** and leader was there to bail them out. **JUST WIN** was still working, and Michigan was heading to the Rose Bowl, and a shot at the National Championship.

So as Michigan prepared for the Rose Bowl and a shot at the National Championship, Charles Woodson would have busy winter break. He was named the team's MVP. He was named All-Big Ten for the third straight season, and a first team All-American. He won the Walter Camp Award (for the College Player of the Year) He also won the Bednarik Award, given to the nation's top defender, and the Jim Thorpe Award, given to the Top Defensive back in the Nation. Woodson was invited to the Downtown Athletic Club in New York, like Desmond Howard 6 years prior. Woodson was named the 1997 Heisman Memorial Trophy winner that night in New York City. He beat out Peyton Manning, a quarterback you may have heard of from Tennessee. Ryan Leaf of Washington State would finish 3rd, and Woodson and Michigan would be taking on Leaf and the Washington State Cougars in the 1998 Rose Bowl.

Woodson was the first primarily defensive player to win the coveted award, but he was certain that his time on the offensive side of the ball didn't hurt. His acceptance speech was gracious, short, and sweet.

1997 HEISMAN VOTING RESULTS

PLACE	NAME	SCHOOL	CLASS	POSITION	1	2	3	TOTAL
1	CHARLES WOODSON*	MICHIGAN	JR.	CB	433	209	98	1815
2	PEYTON MANNING	TENNESSEE	SR.	QB	281	263	174	1543
3	RYAN LEAF	WASHINGTON ST.	JR.	QB	70	203	241	861
4	RANDY MOSS	MARSHALL	SO.	WR	17	56	90	253
5	RICKY WILLIAMS	TEXAS	JR.	RB	3	18	20	65
6	CURTIS ENIS	PENN STATE	JR.	RB	3	18	20	65
7	TIM DWIGHT	IOWA	SR.	RB	5	3	11	32
8	CADE MCNOWN	UCLA	JR.	QB	0	7	12	26
9	TIM COUCH	KENTUCKY	SO.	QB	0	5	12	22
10	AMOS ZEREOUE	WEST VIRGINIA	SO.	RB	3	1	10	21

This **MICHIGAN MAN** knew there was work left to be done, and quickly got back to work, with **JUST WIN** still racing through his mind.

CHARLES WOODSON

2

ATTRIBUTES:

1. NINJA LIKE ATHLETICISM
2. SPEED
3. PHYSICAL ENDURANCE
4. JUST WIN ATTITUDE

THE STATISTICS

PASSING

YEAR	ATTEMPTS	COMP	YARDS	TOUCHDOWNS
1996	1	1	4	0
1997	1	1	28	0
CAREER	2	2	32	0

RUSHING

YEAR	ATTEMPTS	YARDS	AVERAGE	TOUCHDOWNS
1996	6	152	25.3	1
1997	5	21	4.2	1
CAREER	11	173	15.7	2

RECEIVING

YEAR	RECEPTIONS	YARDS	AVERAGE	TOUCHDOWNS
1996	13	164	12.6	1
1997	12	238	19.8	2
CAREER	25	402	16.1	3

PUNT RETURNS

YEAR	RETURNS	YARDS	AVERAGE	TOUCDOWNS
1996	11	106	9.6	0
1997	36	301	8.4	1*
CAREER	47	407	8.7	1

PASS INTERCEPTIONS

YEAR	INTERCEPTIONS	YARDS	AVERAGE	TOUCHDOWNS
1995	5	46	9.2	0
1996	5	28	5.6	0
1997	8	7	0.9	0
CAREER	18	81	4.5	0

OTHER DEFENSIVE STATS

YEAR	TACKLES	TFL	SACKS	PASS BREAKUPS
1995	55	0	0	4
1996	63	0	0	12
1997	44	5	1	9
CAREER	161	5	1	25

ALL CONFERENCE TEAMMATES:

Marcus Ray, Glen Steele, Sam Sword, Andre Weathers, Jerame Tuman Brian Griese, Zach Adami, Steve Hutchinson, Jon Jansen

ALL AMERICAN TEAMMATES:

Glen Steele, Jerame Tuman

INDIVIDUAL AWARDS:

The Heisman Memorial Trophy, The Walter Camp Award, Chevrolet Defensive Player of the Year (2x), Big Ten Defensive Player of the Year Award (2x), Bronco Nagurski Defensive Player of the Year Award, Jim Thorpe Award, 1st Team All-Big Ten (3x), 1st Team All-American

OTHER NOTABLES:

Only primarily defensive player to win the Heisman Memorial Trophy
18 Interceptions over 3 years are still 2nd best all time at Michigan
Lined up at 4 different positions for the Wolverines

THE MOMENT:

Lightning strikes twice, Woodson returns a punt 78 yards for a touchdown against ohio state in 1997, securing the Heisman Memorial Trophy

The stage was set. A defensive minded and blue collared team from Michigan would once again head to Pasadena to play a high scoring, speedy PAC-10 team. They were led by Heisman Trophy Winner Charles Woodson and quarterback Brian Griese. Bob Griese, the Miami Dolphin great and Brian's father would call the game with the legendary Keith Jackson, a Washington State Alum. Goodness, the magic of sports. As I think back at the emotion my father would feel watching me play football, I can only imagine what the famed broadcaster was feeling sitting high above the Rose Bowl, calling a game in which his son was battling for a National Championship.

Washington State struck early on a 15 yard touchdown pass by Ryan Leaf. After a short Michigan possession, Washington State was on the move again. My Dad and I were nervous. Like all Michigan fans, I had seen this happen too many times in Pasadena. The PAC-10 champion was running everywhere, and for a play or two, Michigan looked slow and winded. As Washington State headed down the field for what looked like a 14-0 lead, Superman would save the day again. Leaf threw the ball to an "open" receiver in the left corner of the end zone only to have it snatched out of the air by a leaping Charles Woodson. It was his 8th interception of the season, the season when people were supposed to throw away from his direction. In Leaf's defense, he thought he did. The spark

from their leader was exactly what Michigan needed. The offense came alive, and in the 2nd quarter, Brian Griese hit Tai Streets for a 53 yard touchdown to tie the game at 7 with 7 minutes left in the half.

Leaf would respond on Washington State's first drive of the second half. The 99 yard drive put the Cougars up 13-7. James Hall was able to block the ensuing extra point. Griese found Tai Streets for another touchdown on another play action pass, this time for 58 yards. The play gave Michigan a 14-13 lead. After a defensive stand and punt by Washington State, Griese led another touchdown drive, and finished it with a 23 yard touchdown pass to All-American tight end Jerame Tuman. Washington State would drive later in the 4th quarter for a field goal that brought the score to 21-16 Michigan. Fittingly, it would come down to Woodson and the defense once again. Michigan attempted to run out the clock and had some success. On a 3rd and 7, Michigan would try to squeeze a little more magic out of Woodson. Griese threw a short pass to Woodson, who looked down the field for a double pass. Woodson was the Heisman Trophy winner, the best player in College Football, and the play would cement his place in history. As he gazed down the field and saw everyone covered, I personally think that his own words ran through his mind, **JUST WIN**. With everyone covered, and the maturity of 5th year senior quarterback, he pulled the ball down and ran for 8 yards and a Michigan first down. **MICHIGAN MAN.** The drive would continue, and valuable time was ticking off the clock. He caught another pass on the drive, for 7 more yards and another first down. The drive would eventually end with a pooch punt by Michigan kicker Jay Feely, and Washington State would have one more chance with 16 seconds left on the clock. It would come down to the defense, the only way it should have been in the 1998 Rose Bowl and the 1997 season for Michigan. Leaf completed a 46 yard pass to receiver Nian Taylor to move the ball to the Michigan 47. Following a Washington State penalty, the Cougars would execute a hook and ladder to move the ball to the Michigan 26 yard line. As my Dad and I's hearts started beating a little faster, Washington State was out of timeouts and raced to get off one more play. It didn't happen. Leaf spiked the ball but it was too late. **JUST WIN** and Michigan had held on for their first National Championship since 1947. Woodson and Griese willed the Wolverines to a victory, and Griese would be named the game's Most Valuable Player.

1998 ROSE BOWL

SCORING

		MICH		WSU
First Quarter		22	First Downs	19
WSU	McKenzie 15-yard pass from Leaf (Lindell kick)	41-128	Net Yards Rushing	28-67
		251	Net Yards Passing	331
Second Quarter		63	Total Plays	71
M	Streets, 53-yard Pass form Griese (Baker kick)	379	Total Yards	398
		30/18/1	PA/PC/Int	35/17/1
Third Quarter		6/30.5	Punts/Avg	6/40.3
		1/2	Return Yards	5/56
WSU	Tims 14-yard reverse(Lindell kick blocked)	0/0	Fumbles/Lost	0/0
M	Streets, 58-yard pass from Griese (Baker kick)	4/40	Penalties/Yards	4/43
		32:14	Time of Possession	27:46
Fourth Quarter				
M	Tuman, 23-yard pass from Griese (Baker kick)			
WSU	Lindell field goal, 48-yards			

Rushing— (M): Howard 19-70, Thomas 7-13, C. Williams 2-12, Floyd 4-7, Woodson 2-6, (WSU) Black 7-24, Gilmore 8-20, Tims 1-4, Leaf 10-6, Clayton 2-3

Passing— (M): Griese 18-30-1-251 (WA): Leaf 17-35-1-331

Receiving— (M): Shaw 6-49, Streets 4-127, tuman 2-33, Howard 2-13, Thomas 1-14, Woodson 1-7, campbell 1-7, Williams 1-1 (WSU): Jackson 9-89, McKenzie 5-78, McWashington 2-41, Tims 2-9, Taylor 1-46, Gilmore 1-42, Jefferson 1-8, 1-8

MICHIGAN 21 WASH STATE 16

Michigan would share the National Championship with an undefeated Nebraska team, ughh, but this isn't the forum to discuss a playoff system. To this day my college roommate Sean reminds me to add the "CO" when I talk about Michigan's National Championship. In all, 1997 was one of the greatest seasons in Michigan Football History and they were led by their do it all All-American and Heisman Trophy Winner Charles Woodson. Not since Tom Harmon had there been a Michigan player so menacing and disruptive to opponents on both sides of the ball.

As far as the *"THREE MICHIGAN HEISMAN CRITERIA"* go, Woodson continued the legacy set by Tom Harmon and Desmond Howard. He was a mega recruit, Mr. Football in the State of Ohio. He had options, to include the buckeyes. He was certainly from enemy territory, and broke hearts when he decided to put on the winged helmet and play for Lloyd Carr at Michigan. Like Harmon and Howard, Woodson was at his best against the buckeyes, and never lost to them. He was a part of two upsets in the rivalry, and brought home the Heisman with his punt return touchdown during the game in 1997. In 3 games against the osu, he had 3 interceptions, none bigger than the drive killer to open the 2nd half in 1997.

With a year of eligibility remaining, Charles Woodson entered the 1998 NFL Draft. He was selected 4th overall by the Oakland Raiders. His impact at the professional level was instant. Woodson would be named the NFL Defensive Rookie of the Year. I mentioned earlier that one of his teammates was the other guy who ripped down the East sideline, Desmond Howard. Woodson was selected to the Pro Bowl in consecutive season from 1999-2001. In the 2000 NFL Pro Bowl, Woodson had some interesting company as previously outlined. The roster included so many players who were part of this story: Peyton Manning, Elvis Grbac, Desmond Howard, Eddie George (buckeye Heisman winner), Robert Smith (buckeye), Randy Moss (next to Woodson when the Heisman was announced), Chris Carter (buckeye), Orlando Pace (buckeye), and Derrick Brooks (On Florida State during the 1991 battle at the Big House). Brian Griese was also a Pro Bowler that year although he was injured. There was a major snub in the 2000 Pro Bowl that further ties this story together. Although Elvis Grbac made the Pro Bowl, his go-to receiver for the Chiefs did not. His name? Derrick Alexander, a Michigan #1, who had 1391 yards receiving and 10 touchdowns in 2000. Those numbers were better than a few of the selections that year. The connections amaze me.

Woodson's best teams in Oakland were in 2002 and 2003. The 2003 season ended in the AFC Championship Game against the New England Patriots. The Raiders were ahead, and the Michigan Heisman winner had apparently done it again. He blitzed in and hit Tom Brady, who fumbled, effectively icing the game and a Super Bowl appearance for Oakland. That's right, Tom Brady, another **MICHIGAN MAN** who left the Wolverines after an up and down career to lead the Patriots to Super Bowl titles and continues to play at a high level today. The fumble was reversed, and the controversy of the NFL "Tuck" rule was born. The Patriots won. During 2002, Charles suffered his first major injury of his professional career and was inactive for 8 games. The Raiders still advanced to Super Bowl. Woodson returned for the playoffs but continued to play injured. Despite being less than full speed, he did record an interception in the Super Bowl loss to the Tampa Bay Buccaneers. The 2003 season for the Raiders was not as memorable and the team finished 4-12. During the 2005 season, he broke his leg and only played in six games. Woodson remained in Oakland through 2005, and entered free agency following the season.

Mr. Heisman, like Desmond Howard, would find a home in Green Bay. In 2006, he agreed to terms with the Green Bay Packers for 7 years and 52.7 million dollars. Woodson had reservations about going to Green Bay, I mean come on, it's way up there in Wisconsin, but with his injuries and perceived decline the Packers were the only team offering a contract of that magnitude. In 2006, not only would Woodson take to Green Bay's defense, but he was also the team's primary punt returner. He returned 41 punts for 363 yards. He would also lead the Packers and tie for the NFL lead in interceptions with 8. Packers.com quoted Woodson years later in 2010 declaring that "it was truly a blessing coming to Green Bay." His stellar play in Green Bay continues today. Just to tie my story together he wears #21. He was a key player on 2010's Championship team that last won the Super Bowl when Desmond Howard raced through the Patriots setting Super Bowl records. I think the Packers might be looking for their next **MICHIGAN MAN** right now, and will likely sign any player who wins a Heisman at Michigan forever. If Denard or anybody else finds a way, watch Ted Thompson grab him in the first round. It's really not a bad formula. Forty-five teams have been called Super Bowl Champions in the NFL. 74 percent of these teams have had a **MICHIGAN MAN** on the roster. 13 of those teams have had more than one. There is something about this **MICHIGAN MAN** thing. I can't make this stuff up, check it out. Some were superstars and others reserves, but there is something about having these guys in a locker room.

During the 2011 Super Bowl, Woodson broke his collar bone diving for an interception late in the 2nd quarter. It was a play that further displayed Woodson's unmatched competitiveness and **JUST WIN** attitude. The pass was intended for Mike Wallace of the Steelers. Woodson was in excellent position and covered the play well. Most would have let the ball fall incomplete, but not this guy. He became the receiver and laid out for a spectacular interception. The result was the injury. During the halftime intermission, there was a **MICHIGAN MAN,** giving an inspired speech to his teammates, emotionally outlining what they had come there to do. To play with one goal, one purpose, and one heart….. The Packers did. They prevailed over the Steelers 31-25, with their All-Pro cornerback cheering from the sideline. Like Howard, Woodson now had the Heisman and a Super Bowl Trophy. Unlike Howard however, Woodson also had a National Championship. Woodson was offered and accepted a two year contract extension following the Super Bowl and will likely retire a Green Bay Packer. In 2011, Woodson and the Packers were playoff bound again.

Off the field, Charles Woodson displays a different side. His fierce competitiveness is often replaced with an inherent need to give, insight, and interest in other business ventures. In November 2009 he contributed $2 million to the Mott Children's Hospital at the University of Michigan. He has his own Charity Organization, "The Charles Woodson Foundation," check it out, the Mott donation wasn't a one-time thing (charleswoodsonfoundation.org). They proclaimed April 28th, "Charles Woodson Day." How many pro athletes can say a children's hospital honors their efforts with a day? Not many, but if there were, the world would be a better place. His former Coach and Michigan great Lloyd Carr also supports various charities, and I am sure that some of Carr's lessons rubbed off on Charles off the field as well.

His foundation sponsors golf outings and in 2011 he sponsored one along with Michigan teammates Brian Griese and Steve Hutchinson. Yes, Lloyd Carr even attends. It is actually an annual charity event, put together by Woodson and some **MICHIGAN MEN** to help others. The foundation's website lists some of the participants who played for Michigan to include Tim Biakabutuka, Braylon Edwards, Anthony Carter, Elvis Grbac, and Desmond Howard among others. In addition to the children's hospital the Woodson Foundation raises money and awareness for the fight against breast cancer. In his spare time, Woodson has partnered with a winemaker and developed his own label.

For Woodson, it always has been, and always will be about winning. I wouldn't bet that he approaches charity and the diseases he raises money to fight in any other way. For those of us with loved ones battling these diseases, I don't think there could be a better teammate. **JUST WIN.**

2003-TODAY
THE STORY CONTINUES

2003, CHRIS PERRY # 23

Raymond Christopher Perry was born in 1982 in Advance, North Carolina. Advance is a small town located outside of Winston Salem, North Carolina. You could stumble upon it  looking for Wake Forest, or you could miss it looking for Advance. Michigan coaches actually found Perry after he had left North Carolina and attended Fork Union Military Academy in Virginia. While at Fork Union, Perry was a key player in multiple VISFA State Football Championships.

He took the field for Michigan in 2000, and found a way to make an impact. As a freshman, Perry saw some action. He had 103 yards and a touchdown against Bowling Green after the game was decided in 2000. He would play the rest of the season as a reserve, spelling the "A" Train, Anthony Thomas, another Michigan great. Thomas would run for 1,773 yards on the year while a young Chris Perry would run for 417 and 5 touchdowns.

In 2001, Perry ran for 495 and 2 more touchdowns, but it wasn't what Perry envisioned. He went to Head Coach Lloyd Carr and discussed a transfer. Lloyd was open to it, but at the same time challenged Chris to become a better player, and outlined that he wasn't changing his ways and that there were no stars at Michigan. If Perry didn't like that, he could transfer and play for another team. Sounds very Bo-esque, doesn't it? Lloyd Carr was the total **MICHIGAN MAN.** So there was Perry, with a significant decision to make. At that point, Irene Perry got involved in the situation as only loving mothers can. She spoke to her son as well as the coaches, and moved from the small town outside of Winston Salem, NC to Ann Arbor, Michigan. To be in the company of Tom Harmon, Bill Daley, Ron Johnson, Gordon Bell, Rob Lytle, Butch Woolfolk, Jamie Morris, Tony Boles, Leroy Hoard, Tyrone Whealtley, Tim Biakabutuka, Chris Howard, Anthony Thomas, and more, Perry would have to adjust his attitude. With the support of his mother, he decided to give it a chance. Perry accepted the challenge and would work hard for his role.

When he returned for his junior season, a more dedicated and focused Perry rushed for 1,110 yards and 14 touchdowns. His best games would come against Washington (23 carries for 120 yards and 3 touchdowns, Western Michigan (17 carries for 118 yards), and Wisconsin, (27 carries for 175 yards and a touchdown). His season would culminate with a 4 touchdown effort in the Outback Bowl against Florida. Michigan and Perry were poised for a big 2003 season.

Perry was a senior, and the focal point of Michigan's offense. He was running behind an outstanding MICHIGAN offensive line, no spread option, I mean Michigan. Adam Stenavich, David Baas, Dave Pearson, Matt Lentz, and Tony Pape were opening big holes for Perry. The rest of the offense wasn't too shabby either. The wide receivers were Braylon Edwards (wearing the awarded #1 jersey) and Jason Avant. Tim Massaquoi was the tight end, and John Navarre was under center, a senior quarterback who started 3 years at Michigan. They would open the season with Western Michigan, and Perry was ready to showcase what he could do as a feature back. His patience and decision to stay at Michigan were about to pay off. In the season opener against Central Michigan, Perry ran for 232 yards on 22 carries and two touchdowns. The Wolverines won easily 45-7. The next week brought Houston to the Big House, and

Michigan kept rolling 50-3. Perry gained 184 yards on 27 carries and scored two more touchdowns.

Heading into the annual matchup with Notre Dame Michigan and Chris Perry were becoming the talk of College Football. Thru 3 games, Perry had rushed for 416 yards and 4 touchdowns, following up on his big Bowl performance to end the previous season. Notre Dame wouldn't slow Perry and the Wolverines down. By halftime, Perry eclipsed 500 rushing yards for the season in 2 ½ games, one of only three NCAA players to do so at the time. Perry would score twice in the first half, 1 on a run, and 1 on a catch in front of the record setting crowd of 111,726.

I never actually watched this game until this project. I found a VHS tape that my oldest brother Mike and his wife Joy sent me while I was in Iraq. I had no VCR over there, but still have the tape. Amazingly, it was edited for commercials. If that isn't a big brother's love I don't know what is. Some reading this might not even remember VCRs, but that was something before the days of the DVR. So as I FINALLY watched it, ABC Sports even had an interview with Perry during the game. They asked him about his friendly banter with Michigan wide receiver Braylon Edwards. Both thought they had the best hands on the team, and Perry stated that he had them without question during the interview. During that dominant first half for Michigan Perry would slip out of the backfield on a 3rd and 7, snag a high throw with one hand, control the ball and move up field for 9 yards. What timing. Michigan rolled 38-0, and Perry rushed for another 133 yards and scored 4 total touchdowns.

The following week Michigan suffered their first of two regular season losses. Oregon outgunned the Wolverines 31-27 in Eugene, and the Ducks held Chris Perry to only 26 rushing yards on 11 carries. Yes, it was certainly a setback for Perry's non-promoted Heisman campaign but like I said that is not what it's about at Michigan. It was time to regroup, and Lloyd Carr and the Wolverines were able to. From that loss on the West Coast, Perry and the Wolverines would roll until Iowa. They lost 30-27 to the Hawkeyes. The following week Perry was a key contributor in one of the greatest comebacks in Michigan history on October 10, 2003 at Minnesota in the Metrodome.

Michigan was ranked #4, and Minnesota was ranked #20. It was a dangerous stumbling block for the Wolverines. The Gophers were ready to play in the game that would actually be played on Friday night, broadcast on national television. Minnesota scored first on a run by Marion Barber and then again in the second quarter on a run by Laurence Maroney. Minnesota had two great running backs, and they were on display in 2003. Michigan would finally score in the third quarter to pull within 7, but the initial comeback was short lived. Minnesota scored twice in the quarter and when the 4th quarter began the score was 28-7 Minnesota.

Early in the 4th quarter, Perry would respond with a 10 yard touchdown catch, but Michigan still trailed 28-14. Michigan's defense responded, and Jacob Stewart returned an interception 34 yards to bring the Wolverines within 7.

Minnesota scored again, this time on Asad Abdul-Khaliq's 52 yard run. The memories of Ricky Foggie were stirring up for long time Michigan fans. After another screen to Perry, Michigan went long to Braylon Edwards. His 52 yard score brought the Wolverines within 7 again at 28-35 with 10:18 left in the game. It was a wild quarter in Minneapolis. With 5:48 remaining, Perry found the end zone again, this time on a 10 yard run. With 47 seconds remaining in the game, Michigan would complete the comeback. Garret Rivas hit a 33 yard field goal to put Michigan ahead for good 38-35. Perry ran for 85 yards and a touchdown on the day, but it was his receiving once again that kept Michigan in the game. Perry had 11 catches for 121 yards, and the ten yard touchdown. It was perhaps the greatest comeback in Michigan history, Perry along with John Navarre and Braylon Edwards shined. In the Michigan State game, on the road, Perry would display incredible toughness and endurance. In a hard fought 27-20 win, Perry carried the ball **51** times for 219 yards and scored a touchdown.

Perry entered the annual matchup with ohio state with 1,535 yards rushing and 15 touchdowns. Ohio state was ranked

#6 and Michigan was ranked #4. Once again the Big Ten
Title was at stake. Michigan struck early. In an 18 play, 89
yard drive with lots of Chris Perry, WR/Everything man
Steve Breaston would provide the first touchdown on a 3
yard run from the quarterback position. Before halftime
Perry contributed several key runs and first down, as WR
Braylon Edwards sliced through the buckeye defense with two
touchdowns. Ohio state scored 44 seconds before halftime to
make the score 21-7 Wolverines. In the second half,
Michigan would put the game in Chris Perry's and the
offensive line's hands again. He scored from 30 yards out
during the first drive after halftime, on a memorable run in
which he started up the middle, stopped an osu linebacker in
his tracks, cut left, headed down the sideline, and finally
into the end zone diving into the left pylon. The buckeyes
responded with two more touchdowns, but Perry would ice
the game with a 15 yard score in the famed east corner of the
end zone to seal a 35-21 victory over Jim Tressel and ohio
state. Perry ran for 154 yards on 31 carries, along with the
two touchdowns.

Although he would not win the Heisman, Perry's
dream season is one for Michigan fans to remember. It was
a story of hard work and perseverance. Perry placed 4th in the
Heisman Memorial Trophy Voting, and Michigan went on to
face USC in the Rose Bowl once again. In addition to
placing 4th in Heisman Voting, Perry was the first Michigan

running back to win the Doak Walker Award as the Nation's Top Running Back. He was also a consensus All-American and the Big Ten Offensive Player of the year and MVP. Michigan lost in the Rose Bowl 28-14 to USC and Heisman candidate Matt Leinart. What is with that place? Perry scored once rushing for 85 yards on 23 carries. He rushed for 1,674 and 18 touchdowns for the year, averaging 5 yards per carry. As far as the *"THREE MICHIGAN HEISMAN CRITERIA"* Perry probably finished 1/3. He wasn't a mega recruit, and was certainly not from Big Ten enemy territory. He was however one of the LAST known buckeye killers to wear the maize and blue until 2011. His 12 one hundred yard career rushing games rank 10th in Michigan history, and his season total ranks 5th all-time at Michigan. His 51 carries against Michigan State are still the Michigan record, and he scored 39 rushing touchdowns, good for 4th all time for the Wolverines. His development from near transfer to **MICHIGAN MAN** is one of the great stories in Michigan Football History, and a testament to Perry and Coach Lloyd Carr. Perry would move on to the NFL and was drafted by the Cincinnati Bengals in the first round of the 2004 NFL draft. Perry had his best season in 2005 when he rushed for 279 yards and also had 328 yards receiving and two touchdowns serving as the backup to Pro Bowl back Rudi Johnson. His best football days were at Michigan in 2003.

2003 HEISMAN VOTING RESULTS

PLACE	NAME	SCHOOL	CLASS	POSITION	1	2	3	TOTAL
1	JASON WHITE	OKLAHOMA	JR.	QB	319	204	116	1481
2	LARRY FITZGERALD	PITTSBURGH	SO.	WR	253	233	128	1353
3	ELI MANNING	MISSISSIPPI	SR.	QB	95	132	161	710
4	CHRIS PERRY*	MICHIGAN	SR.	RB	27	66	128	341
5	DARREN SPROLES	KANSAS STATE	SR.	RB	15	30	29	134
6	MATT LEINART	USC	SO.	QB	5	27	58	127
7	PHILLIP RIVERS	N.C. STATE	SR.	QB	18	20	24	118
8	MIKE WILLIAMS	USC	SR.	WR	12	12	18	78
9	BEN ROTHLISBERGER	MIAMI (OHIO)	JR.	QB	5	9	14	47
10	B.J. SYMONS	TEXAS TECH	JR.	QB	1	7	21	38

Perry was injured with a fractured leg, in 2006 and finally released by the Bengals in 2009.

2004, BRAYLON EDWARDS # 1

Braylon Jamel Edwards was born on February 21st, 1983 in Detroit, Michigan. He attended Bishop Gallagher High School. He is the son of a **MICHIGAN MAN.** His father Stan Edwards was a running back who played for Michigan from 1977-1981 who rushed for over 2,200 yards and scored

16 career touchdowns. As Edwards developed as a high school athlete, it was pretty clear he was born to be at Michigan. He arrived at Michigan in 2001 and played sparingly as a freshman. That season he appeared in two games and had 3 catches for 38 yards.

#80 at the time would return for his sophomore season with a year under his belt and began to contribute on a much larger level. He was splitting time with Tyrece Butler, Ronald Bellamy, and Calvin Bell. He opened that season with a strong 5 catch, 80 yard, and 1 touchdown performance against Washington. From there Edwards continued to grow and develop as wide receiver in the Big Ten. He had four 100 yard receiving regular season games. During the same Outback Bowl against Florida, while Chris Perry scored 4 touchdowns for the Wolverines, Braylon Edwards had 4 catches for 110 yards and a long of 49. Michigan finished the season 10-3, and #80 amassed 67 catches for 1,035 yards and 10 touchdowns. Following the season, and heading into 2003, he even approached his coaches about changing numbers. He WANTED # 1. Growing up a Wolverine, he was well aware of the tradition and the significance. After a productive offseason and a great fall camp, Braylon Edwards got his wish. He was wearing the # 1 jersey at Michigan, and was ready to show the world why.

So while Chris Perry ran through the Big Ten in 2003, Edwards was stretching the field in a much different way. The friendly debate about who had the better hands was the background to a great performance by the two developing Michigan stars. Edwards opened the 2003 season with 2 touchdowns against Central Michigan. In the losing effort at Oregon, Edwards was a bright spot for Michigan with 144 yards receiving on 13 receptions. At Iowa, # 1 had 7 catches for 114 yards and 2 touchdowns. In the Michigan State game when Perry carried the ball 51 times, it was Edwards with 2 touchdowns and 103 yards receiving at Spartan Stadium.

Then, against ohio state, he put on a show. In the 2ⁿᵈ quarter, John Navarre found Edwards on touchdowns of 64 and 23 yards. The first was a play in which he caught the ball in the middle of the field, sliced through the buckeyes and headed down that same east sideline where Desmond Howard and Charles Woodson gashed buckeye hopes in previous years. The second catch was in the end zone as he caught the ball among several defenders. In the 3ʳᵈ quarter, he had apparently scored again on an 84 yard touchdown, but the play would be called back due to a holding penalty. It didn't matter. Edwards had done plenty to contribute to the Wolverines last victory over the school from the south until 2011, and finished the game with 130 yards receiving and 2 touchdowns on 7 catches. In the Rose Bowl loss to eventual

National Champion USC, Edwards had another 100 yard performance. He was All Big Ten as a junior, and poised for a big year in 2004 despite the fact that Chris Perry, John Navarre, and a host of others were moving on.

So there was Edwards, on everybody's preseason All- American teams, and even a few Heisman watch lists, but who was going to throw him the ball? The answer surprised most, to include us Michigan fans. Matt Gutierrez was thought to be the next in line after John Navarre, but the staff saw something in true freshman Chad Henne. The season opener was against Miami of Ohio. Michigan would start a true freshman quarterback, like Rick Leach, and Henne was up to the task. During the 43-10 Michigan victory, it was clear that Henne had already figured out what so many Michigan quarterbacks had over the years since Anthony Carter. "Throw it to the guy wearing # 1!" Edwards scored twice on 6 catches and had 91 yards receiving. The following week Michigan fell to Notre Dame in South Bend. He recorded 12 catches for 129 yards in the losing effort, but the final score was 28-20 ND.

The Wolverines rallied, and still made 2004 a memorable season. San Diego State came to the Big House the following week, and Michigan got things together. Henne found Edwards 8 times to the tune of 130 yards and two more touchdowns. Being a freshman starter at quarterback in the Big Ten is tough, but it's a little easier with #1 on the receiving end. The following week they faced Iowa, and the two connected for another 150 yards and a touchdown. Michigan went to Indiana the following week, and the senior receiver put on a show. 8 catches, 165 yards, and 2 more touchdowns as Michigan started gaining momentum as a team. Michigan kept rolling and the Spartans came to Michigan Stadium on October 30th, 2004.

I will never forget that day. I was stationed at Fort Bragg, NC, as well as my older brother Mark. At the time he was a Captain, and I was a 2nd Lieutenant. Let me first give you a little background on my brother and I. I had spent my whole life battling him 1 on 1 in the driveway, and we even got to serve with each other in the Army. He was older and wiser, but we were both incredibly competitive. We both went to the Big House growing up, and cheered for the Wolverines in Ann Arbor and Chicago. The same guy throwing me Desmond fades is the guy that taught me how to play basketball. We played for years, and the results were the same. Mike Hart once talked about "little brother" to the Spartans, and I have to laugh. Mark was 6'3" tall and a great athlete. I was 5'9" and trying to be like my big brother. We battled often in Wheaton, Illinois and as I got older the games got more competitive.

Finally, as an aspiring freshman in high school, the stars would align. Mark was a heading to Michigan State, where he was going to play club volleyball for the Spartans.

He was coming home for the daily rematch after a workout and was certainly tired. Taking advantage of the situation, for the first and only time, I won. If I could take it all back, I don't think I would, but let's just say it might not have been the best decision to stand on my Dad's ladder and cut down the net in the driveway. Before I could extend my hand for an insincere good game, he was ticked and heading in, and I was calling my buddy Doug. Mark and I have an amazing bond from that driveway to some wild times in the 82nd Airborne, but in some ways I don't think the competition will ever die because of the Spartans and Wolverines. I am, the "little brother," depending on how you define it (see the Mike Hart section for further explanation on LITTLE BROTHER). On one of my first parachute jumps in the 82nd, there we were again. We jumped next to each other. When I saw him on the drop zone, there was my brother. He had a big Desmond smile and a Gatorade. I had actually only brought water in canteens. My brother was still teaching me lessons and watching over me, Spartan or not☺

So the Spartans and Wolverines were playing, and my brother and his wife were coming over with the kids. To say they were anti-Michigan would be an understatement. Not only was my brother a Spartan graduate, and proud to be, but my sister-in-law Jen played women's volleyball at Notre Dame on scholarship. Mark showed up in his Tony Bank's #12 Spartan jersey, and I of course was sporting the

Heisman #21. Mark had bailed on Michigan long before, and I think there is even a class at Michigan State, developed from the one at osu that teaches you how to discount the Wolverines as spoiled and arrogant. My Spartan brothers only received 1 credit hour each for the course, but at osu I heard you get 3 and possibly even a minor.

So Michigan was moving up the ranks with an 8-1 record, and the Spartans were 4-4. Before the game even started, I was hearing about Michigan's lone loss to Notre Dame, the one during which my niece who was learning to talk proudly declared "Go Irish," clear as could be.

The Spartans came out fighting and would quickly take a 14-7 lead on 72 yard run by Deandra Cobb and a 5 yard run by QB Drew Stanton. The teams exchanged field goals and the Spartans led 17-10 at the half. Oh that was a long halftime. I could feel the quiet confidence of my Spartan brother and I was stewing. The teams would battle scoreless in the third quarter, and the fireworks were about to start. Michigan State converted a field goal, and then Deandra Cobb (22 carries for 205 yards) would explode for his second long scoring run, this time for 64 yards. My usually reserved and mostly good sported brother exploded into a dance in the town house living room. I was sick. Things weren't looking good for Michigan, but Braylon Jamel Edwards was about to show why he was given the # 1.

Trailing 27-10 with 8:43 left in the game, Michigan was just getting started. They converted a field goal, and then recovered an onside kick. When they got the ball back, and # 1 was finally able to get open. Freshman quarterback Chad Henne found Edwards for 36 yards in the right corner of the end zone on a play where a Spartan defender had perfect position but Edwards elevated and wrestled the ball away for the score. The Big House was in a frenzy as the Wolverines pulled within 7. Quietly, against the norm, I sat on the couch, nervous and knowing there was more work to be done. Typically I am the guy dancing around the living room. There was 6:12 remaining in the game and Cobb and the Spartans were going to get the ball back. The Michigan defense held. Mike Hart broke loose on a long run down the left sideline and Michigan was on the move again. From the Spartan 21 yard line Henne would "throw to # 1" again. Edwards once again out jumped a Spartan cornerback with an acrobatic catch to tie the score after the extra point.

I was done being nervous and shouted with joy and the excitement of another Big House miracle. The game was heading into overtime. Michigan got the ball first, and only converted field goal. My stomach sank again. The defense held and MSU kicked a field goal. The game was heading to double overtime tied at 30. The Spartans got the ball first in the 2nd overtime, and running back Jason Teague would score on a three yard run. The pressure swung toward

Michigan. They responded with Chad Henne, growing up with each and every play that season, and he found Jason Avant for a 5 yard touchdown pass. It was another amazing catch by a Michigan receiver on that day. In the third overtime, Michigan would finally prevail. Fittingly, it was Braylon Edwards on a slant crossing the field with 4 Spartans in the vicinity, scoring the Michigan touchdown. Michigan converted the two point conversion. The Spartan's final attempt fell incomplete. Mark and I would hug before they packed up to go, but for about 30 tense minutes, we might as well have been back in the driveway in Wheaton, with a tension only sports can provide. Edwards finished the day with 11 catches for 189 yards and his 3 scores were in the 4th quarter and overtime.

Edwards was having an All-Big Ten and All-American season but there was work left to be done. Michigan was heading to play ohio state. The game was in Columbus, and they were ready for revenge after the Chris Perry/Braylon Edwards show of 2003. The buckeyes got their wish. Michigan this time would have their season spoiled by their arch rival. Osu stars Troy Smith (2006 Heisman Trophy Winner) and Ted Ginn, Jr would put their first marks on the series, and the Wolverines fell 37-21 at the horseshoe. Edwards had a big game, 11 catches for 172 yards and 1 touchdown, but it wasn't enough. Despite the loss Michigan

still moved on to face Texas in the Rose Bowl as the Big Ten
Champion.

The Wolverines eventually fell to Texas (led by
2005 Heisman Trophy Winner Vince Young). In a back and
forth Rose Bowl with plenty of fireworks, Braylon Edwards
caught 10 passes for 109 yards and three touchdowns. In the
end Michigan lost 38-37 on a late field goal. Michigan's
defense had no answers for Vince Young, which would be
the theme for College Football in 2005. Edwards finished
his career with several Michigan receiving records, and was
named the 2004 Fred Biletnikoff Award winner for the
nation's best receiver. He was also the Big Ten Offensive
Player of the Year. # 1 was dominant and had a knack for
playing his best when the Wolverines needed him the most.
Edwards finished 10th in the Heisman Voting in 2004, with
USC and Oklahoma players dominating the votes while
battling for the National Championship.

2004 HEISMAN TROPHY VOTING RESULTS

PLACE	NAME	SCHOOL	CLASS	POSITION	1	2	3	TOTAL
1	MATT LEINART	USC	JR.	QB	267	211	102	1325
2	ADRIAN PETERSON	OKLAHOMA	SO.	RB	154	180	175	997
3	JASON WHITE	OKLAHOMA	SR.	QB	171	149	146	957
4	ALEX SMITH	UTAH	SR.	QB	98	112	117	635
5	REGGIE BUSH	USC	SO.	RB	118	80	83	597
6	CEDRIC BENSON	TEXAS	SR.	RB	12	41	69	187
7	JASON CAMPBELL	AUBURN	SR.	QB	21	24	51	162
8	J.J. ARRINGTON	CALIFORNIA	SR.	RB	10	33	19	115
9	AARON RODGERS	CALIFORNIA	JR.	QB	8	14	15	67
10	BRAYLON EDWARDS*	MICHIGAN	SR.	WR	3	13	27	62

When he left Michigan, Edwards had certainly justified his donning of the # 1 jersey, and did his part to continue building that tradition. Edward's receiving yards in a career (3541), season (1,330), and 39 career touchdown receptions are all Michigan records to this day. His 15 touchdowns in a season rank second on to Desmond Howard's 19, and his 189 yard performance against Michigan State in 2004 still ranks 3rd all time. As far as the *"THREE MICHIGAN HEISMAN CRITERIA"* go, Edwards also came close. Although Edwards was from Detroit, he was also a mega recruit, and gets some credit as one of the last known buckeye killers until the streak broke in 2011. Although he and the Wolverines fell to their rival in 2004, Edwards put on a show in 2003. Edwards was born a **MICHIGAN MAN**, and came to Ann Arbor and backed it up with his play on the field.

After his days at Michigan, Edwards moved on to the NFL in the 2005 NFL draft. Braylon was selected # 3 overall by the Cleveland Browns. He had 512 yards and 3 touchdowns in his injury shortened rookie season. In his second NFL season, he would have 61 receptions for 884 yards. In 2007, Edwards became the first Brown's receiver to make the Pro Bowl since 1989 when he had 1289 receiving yards and 16 touchdowns. Both were Cleveland Brown's records.

Edwards then played for the New York Jets, after being traded by the Browns. There have been several controversial reports about Edwards since he left Michigan ranging from disputes with teammates, speeding tickets, and even a DWI. Through it all however, Braylon Jamel Edwards remains a **MICHIGAN MAN** at heart. In 2005, Edwards donated a large sum of money back to the University of Michigan. He sponsors a scholarship that is associated with the #1 jersey he so desperately wanted to wear. In 2006, he struck a deal with some middle school students who would be entering high school the next year in Cleveland. He said that if they maintained a certain GPA, and performed fifteen hours of community service he would pay for their college education. On May 25th, 2011, Edwards, no longer a Brown, agreed to honor his promise. The Sporting News captured these comments from Edwards, via Twitter:

"As the 2nd most hated man in Cleveland, and a man of my word, today I will honor a promise I made 100 students in Cleveland years ago, those of my Advance 100 students will graduate from my program and head off to college on scholarships that I will provide them with. Guys, enjoy and embrace your new beginnings and remember your promise to me, to reach back and help someone else along the way."

Say what you want about Mr. Edwards, and any controversy he has been associated with. The most defining characteristic of this **MICHIGAN MAN**, like Woodson, might be his heart. You can look up the Braylon Edwards Foundation online (www.braylonedwardsfoundation.org), the opening page says "Receiving Means Giving." He sponsors charity events throughout the year, while attending others like the golf tournament sponsored by Woodson, Hutchinson, and Griese. Lloyd Carr taught a lot more than football, and Edwards is more proof. In 2011, Braylon Edwards played for the San Francisco 49ers and another **MICHIGAN MAN**, Head Coach Jim Harbaugh, before being cut while battling injuries.

2006, MIKE HART # 20

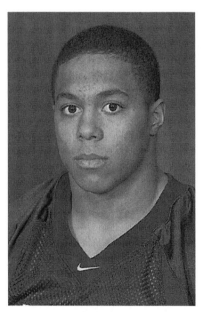

Leon "Michael" Hart was born in Syracuse, New York where he was a standout athlete for Onondaga Central High School. He was the player of the year in the Class D and Class C divisions of New York State High School Football. During his career, his team would win 3 State Titles. His high school numbers were amazing,

11,232 yards on 935 carries to go with the national record for touchdowns in a high school career with 204. He also managed 47 consecutive 100 yard rushing games. In his senior year alone he scored 67 total touchdowns. He even managed to be the point guard on the basketball team, and averaged 10 points and five rebounds. He wasn't the prototypical size to be a running back in the Big Ten (5'9", around 190 as a freshman), but he arrived in Ann Arbor with quite a resume.

It didn't take long for Hart to make an impact. While the Michigan world was surprised that Chad Henne would be the opening day starter in 2004, another true freshman, #20 was getting a few carries early in the season and raising some eyebrows. Against Miami (Ohio) Hart managed 20 yards on his first 3 collegiate carries. Against San Diego State, Hart ran for 121 yards on 25 carries, and established himself as Michigan's #1 option at tailback. Against Iowa, Hart would score his first touchdown at Michigan and account for 99 total yards in the Wolverines 30-17 win at the Big House.

Over the next 4 weeks, Mike Hart began to showcase more in support of the Wolverines. He had 160 yards against Minnesota, 234 at Illinois, 206 at Purdue, and 225 in the triple overtime thriller against Michigan State at the Big House. It was pretty clear who Michigan's running back was at that point. Against Northwestern the following week on November 13th, 2004, Hart would find the end zone 3 times while rushing for 151 yards.

The ohio state game in 2004 was the first setback since Notre Dame, as outlined under Braylon Edwards. Michigan fell 37-21. Hart did score in the game, but was held to 61 yards rushing on 18 carries. Despite the disappointing end to the 2004, Michigan moved on to the Rose Bowl, and lost to Texas and the "Vince Young Show." For his performance throughout the season, Mike Hart was named the Big Ten Freshman of the year, and led the Big Ten in rushing. Michigan had answered two major questions in 2004, and had a quarterback and running back ready to continue their dominance in 2005.

With the nucleus of the team returning, Michigan entered the 2005 season ranked # 3 in the nation, and most would agree why not? They opened the season against Northern Illinois, and Mike Hart picked right up where he left off as a freshman in 2004. Hart rushed for 117 yards and a touchdown, as Michigan struggled early but went on to win 33-17. Michigan's National Title hopes were all but extinguished the following week. Notre Dame came to the Big House with a big time signal caller in Brady Quinn, and a brand new scheme orchestrated by Head Coach Charlie Weis. Hart was injured in the game and managed only 3 carries for 4 yards. Not only had Michigan dropped an early season game, but they lost the "Hart" of the offense for most of the game. Sorry, I couldn't resist. Notre Dame prevailed 17-10, and Michigan was 1-1 heading into a home game against Eastern Michigan. They fell to # 14 in the polls and would be without #20's services for a few weeks. Michigan handled the Eastern Michigan Eagles 55-0, and their next game was at Wisconsin.

Michigan went to Camp Randall Stadium and dropped their second game of the season 23-20 to the #24 ranked Badgers. Wisconsin utilized a 17 point 4th quarter to upset the Wolverines. The Wolverines failed to score on the goal line after a 96 yard drive that would have sealed the game. An injured Mike Hart had to stand and watch as the offense couldn't close out the drive. Hart was fierce competitor, but that day he could only watch.

20 returned to the lineup the following week against the Michigan State Spartans in East Lansing. Wolverine fans were glad he did. He contributed 218 yards and a touchdown on 36 carries to the Michigan 34-31 upset win in overtime over the #12 ranked Michigan State Spartans. That would be one of the few highlights for the Wolverines the rest of the way in 2005. Although Michigan was able to upset Penn State on a touchdown pass from Chad Henne to Mario Manningham as time expired (Hart rushed for 108 yards and 1 touchdown) they would lose to Minnesota at home, ohio state at home, and to Nebraska in the Alamo Bowl. Hart spent the year on and off the injury

report, and finished the season with 662 yards and only 4 touchdowns. The timely first down runs, pass protection, and touchdowns they counted on from the 5'9" back from Syracuse were missing, and the Wolverines felt it.

2006 was brand new year for an angry and motivated Michigan team. Lloyd Carr was able to refocus the Wolverines. He had plenty of examples of what went wrong from 2005, and the 2006 Wolverines would play with passion, motivation, and a serious chip on their shoulder. They were ranked #14 with plenty of talent, but who could forget 2005? Lloyd Carr and the Wolverines did.

Week one brought Vanderbilt. It was the home opener for the Wolverines. Michigan beat Vanderbilt 27-7 showcasing a powerful defense and a balanced offense. With a healthy Mike Hart, and Chad Henne still under center, 2006 looked like a different story. Hart ran for 146 yards in the victory. The following week Michigan faced Central Michigan at the Big House, and won easily 41-17. The offense remained balanced, and #20 rushed for another 116 yards and scored 3 touchdowns. Michigan was heading to Notre Dame ranked #13 and facing the #3 ranked Fighting Irish. Notre Dame was the talk of College Football at the time under Charlie Weis, and was coming off a 41-17 victory over Penn State. Brady Quinn (# 3 in the Heisman voting in 2006) was throwing the ball all over the field and Michigan had their work cut out for them.

I learned on that day that the best way to beat a great team is to never give them a chance. It's not very often that it happens, but on September 16th, 2006 Michigan did just that. On the opening drive, Michigan linebacker Prescott Burgess intercepted Brady Quinn and returned it 31 yards for the game's first points. Notre Dame scored a touchdown, but it was all Michigan from there. The balanced attack left Notre Dame without answers as the defense kept attacking. Hart would run for 124 yards and a touchdown, but the story of the game was the Chad Henne to Mario Manningham connection that Notre Dame couldn't stop. Notre Dame had to account for Mike Hart and the running game, and Michigan took full advantage of it. The two would connect for touchdowns of 69, 20, and 22 yards before halftime and Michigan prevailed 47-21. The 47 points were the most the Irish had surrendered at home since 1960, and Michigan had made their official response to the media expecting more from them in 2005. 2006 was going to be different.

The next two weeks were about avenging more losses from the previous season. Michigan would win at home against Wisconsin and at Minnesota. Hart had 91 yards and a touchdown against Wisconsin, and 195 at Minnesota. The following week brought Michigan State, and Michigan's dominance continued. The Wolverines led 17-0 at the half, and would go on to win 31-13. Henne and Manningham were at work again, and Hart added 122 yards on the ground. The Spartans scored twice in the second half to make it look closer than it was, but for Michigan it was about winning and moving on.

A showdown against Penn State in Happy Valley came next. Michigan's defense was dominant with 7 sacks. In the process, Michigan knocked both the first and second string quarterbacks out of the game, and Mike Hart and the offense did the rest. #20 ran for 112 yards and another touchdown. Michigan was ranked #3. Iowa came to the Big House on October 21, 2006. Hart would pace the Wolverines once again with another 100 yard effort. 126 yards to be exact, with 2 more touchdowns. At that time, Hart was even being considered a Heisman Trophy candidate in the media. He was a leader and his consistency made the Wolverines go.

The next two weekends were home wins against Northwestern and a Ball State team coached by Brady Hoke. Hoke and Ball State gave Michigan a scare. The final score was 34-26, but Hart wouldn't let Michigan fail, and ran for 154 yards on 25 carries and scored a touchdown. The once **MICHIGAN MAN** and current Head Coach of the Wolverines was in the process of turning around his alma mater. He gave the Wolverines a scare, but Michigan survived and moved on to play Indiana on the road. What could have been a stumbling block turned out to be another day at the office for the Wolverines. Michigan defeated

Indiana 34-3. Hart ran for another 92 yards and a touchdown, and the stage was set for what will forever be known as **THE GAME.**

Heading into the Michigan and ohio state matchup in 2006, **THE GAME** had never been bigger. For the first time ever, arguably the greatest rivalry in sports had a unique situation. Ohio state was ranked #1 and Michigan was ranked #2. Ohio state was led by Heisman candidate Troy Smith, Ted Ginn Jr, Chris "Beanie" Wells, and an equally stout defense. The game would be played in Columbus, and the world would be watching.

The night before **THE GAME** news spread that would change the Michigan Football world forever. Glenn Edward "Bo" Schembechler had passed away. He was the biggest figure in Michigan Football history, and it all started in 1969 with an upset win over ohio state. When the word came out that Bo had passed, that game took on whole new meaning. Bo was ohio state's legendary coach Woody Hayes' assistant that would go on to battle with Woody during the 10 year war as the Coach of the Wolverines. Amazingly, during that week, Bo Schembechler spoke to a Michigan TEAM one last time. Bo wasn't doing well, and Lloyd Carr even advised him that he didn't need to speak to the team. Bo decided that he would. So as Bo stood and spoke to the team for the last time, fans everywhere prepared for **THE GAME**.

I remember the day well. My father had called me, and I was at work and of course "busy." He called again, and I knew I had missed something. When I got off I quickly called my Dad back and he told me to check ESPN, and that the legendary Bo Schembechler, one of my Dad's heroes had passed. I got home and jumped on the internet. I watched ESPN and anything else I could find. How could this be before one of the biggest games in Michigan Football history? It was tragic and meant to be at the same time. The coverage was amazing. Whether you loved the buckeyes or the Wolverines, the story of Woody and Bo was back at the front. The rivalry, the friendship, and most importantly the respect. The hate cast between Michigan and ohio state fans was set aside for one moment, and the College Football world remembered one of the greatest on November 16th-17th, 2006. Bo was 77. Neither Michigan nor ohio state (the lower case throughout is all for you Bo) needed any extra incentive, but the events would take the 2006 match-up to even another level. The man who brought so many great players and coaches to Michigan, the man who put Michigan back on the map, and the man that upset his mentor to start the war in 1969 had passed on the eve of **THE GAME.**

When I talked to my Father again later, I could hear the emotion in his voice. He had met Bo on a few occasions while teaching ROTC at Michigan, and even wrote a poem for Bo's retirement. He presented the original "Ode to Bo" in 1989 personally and for the Gallaghers it was a sad, sad, day along with the rest of the Michigan world. After a long phone conversation about our days in Ann Arbor, Bo, and those who followed, my Dad and I looked forward to kick off with rest of the College Football world and the entire Michigan Football community. Prior to the game there was a moment of silence for Bo. It was a moment that defined the great rivalry. It was respectful and emotional, like the relationship of the two men who made the rivalry what it is today. Woody and Bo were certainly both watching proudly in some way, and more ready for the kickoff than any player on the field.

So with the hype over, it was time to play **THE GAME**. Hart and the Wolverines got the ball first. The first play went to Hart, and then the Henne to Mannigham connection would quickly connect for 24 yards. Michigan kept the balance that led to their success all year. Short passes followed runs by #20. Henne and Manninghan connected for another 25 yards down to the 1 yard line. Hart scored easily from the 1 and Michigan led 7-0.

Troy Smith and the buckeye offense responded quickly. Ohio state was operating out of a spread look and put the ball in the air early and often on November 17th, 2006. They spread Michigan's powerful defense across the field, and forced them to play an additional defensive back for most of the game. Smith found Roy Hall in the right corner of the end zone to tie the score at 7. Henne missed a wide open Mario Manningham on the next drive, a drive that would eventually stall. Michigan's defense also got a stop, and the first quarter would end at 7-7. Early in the 2nd quarter, the scarlet and gray took control. Chris "Beanie" Wells, the outstanding true freshman running back scored from 52 yards out. The offense wasn't moving the ball, and osu was attacking the Michigan defense. Troy Smith found Ted Ginn on a 37 yard touchdown on a play action fake. It was 21-7 ohio state, and things weren't going well in Columbus for Hart and the Wolverines.

Chad Henne found Adrian Arrington for a 39 yard touchdown, and Michigan pulled within 21-14. Osu came right back down the field and scored, Troy Smith to Anthony Gonzales. The Wolverines trailed 28-14 at the half. None of us fans will ever know what was said at halftime, but Michigan wasn't going to go down easy. The second half started with a healthy dose of #20, Michael Hart.

Michigan's first possession of the 2nd half would be a matter of will. Hart ran through a tackle attempt by buckeye superstar James Laurinaitis. The next play Hart took the ball down the left sideline for 33 yards before being pushed out of bounds. Hart again, and he blasted for 20 more yards, this time down to the 2 yard line. Hart carried it again, this time for a touchdown as he stiff armed a defender to the ground crossing the goal line. That drive to me, was an excellent summary of Mike Hart's time at Michigan. When the Wolverines needed him the most, Hart willed the Wolverines back into the game. Things were getting interesting.

Michigan defensive tackle Alvin Branch picked off Troy Smith on the ensuing drive. Michigan had the ball inside the buckeye 30 yard line, but had to settle for a field goal by Garrett Rivas and pulled to within 28-24.   Osu came back in a big way. Antonio Pittman took a handoff and scored from 56 yards out. Michigan trailed 35-24, and would be forced to punt again on the ensuing drive. As the teams battled on, Brent Musberger even threw Mike Hart's name into the Heisman discussion with Troy Smith and Brady Quinn of Notre Dame. He was throwing his name in conditionally, that "if Hart and the Wolverines could somehow pull out a victory" than the little guy would be in the conversation. It was Michigan's turn to recapture the momentum. To open the 4th quarter, Steve Breaston scored on a reverse. The officials ruled he was down at the one yard line after a replay review. Mike Hart would power the ball over the goal line again, blasting through two buckeye defenders. It wasn't a secret to anyone in the stadium who would get the ball, but #20 would not be denied.   Michigan trailed 35-31.

The teams battled back and forth, but in the end, Michigan's comeback attempt would fall short. Ohio state played a great game. They spread the field and kept

Michigan off balance most of the day. On a late touchdown drive, osu would be given one last chance to finish off the Wolverines. They were aided by a questionable call on a 3rd and 15 when Shawn Crable hit Troy Smith as he released a pass right near the right sideline and the flag came flying. Instead of a long field goal attempt, they were back in business and would score another touchdown on that drive. After the game there was even talk of rematch for the National Championship, similar to the discussions that have led to LSU and Alabama II in 2011-2012. It wouldn't happen, but **THE GAME** was one that actually lived up to all the hype. Michigan made no excuses. The field was replaced before the game, Bo, and even some calls that ultimately affected the outcome. I certainly had some excuses and complaints, but not my Wolverines. Michigan went to the Rose Bowl and lost to USC and their Heisman Candidate Dwayne Jarrett (9th place in 2006).

2006 HEISMAN TROPHY VOTING RESULTS

PLACE	NAME	SCHOOL	CLASS	POSITION	1	2	3	TOTAL
1	TROY SMITH	OHIO STATE	SR.	QB	801	62	13	2540
2	DARREN MCFADDEN	ARKANSAS	SO.	RB	45	298	147	878
3	BRADY QUINN	NOTRE DAME	SR.	QB	13	276	191	782
4	STEVE SLATON	WEST VIRGINIA	SO.	RB	6	51	94	214
5	MIKE HART*	MICHIGAN	JR.	RB	5	58	79	210
6	COLT BRENNAN	HAWAII	JR.	QB	6	44	96	202
7	RAY RICE	RUTGERS	SO.	RB	1	16	44	79
8	IAN JOHNSON	BOISE STATE	JR.	RB	1	13	44	73
9	DWAYNE JARRETT	USC	JR.	WR	1	11	22	47
10	CALVIN JOHNSON	GEORGIA TECH	JR.	WR	1	8	24	43

The buckeyes lost to the Florida Gators in the National Championship Game. Hart was selected to the All-Big Ten team, along with several Wolverine teammates. Hart had his best season in 2006 as a Wolverine running for 1,562 yards and 14 touchdowns. Troy Smith did take home College Football's greatest individual award, and Hart finished 5th.

Michigan looked like a National Title contender once again in 2007 and was ranked #5 in the preseason polls. Unfortunately, 2007 wouldn't be what Michigan hoped. They dropped the first two games. Appalachian State came to Big House on September 1st, 2007 and left with perhaps the greatest upset victory in the history of College Football. After struggling against the Mountaineers all day, Michigan took a brief lead in the 4th quarter 32-31, on an amazing run by their leader Mike Hart. Hart ran for 188 yards and 3 touchdowns on the day, but it wasn't enough.

Michigan also lost at home to Oregon. Although Michigan would rebound, but 2007 definitely wasn't the chase for the National Championship they envisioned. Hart had another impressive season, rushing for 1,419 yards and 14 more touchdowns. Hart provided some memories, running hard throughout 2007 while battling injuries again. He was a fierce competitor and made news following the Michigan State game by referring to the Spartans as Michigan's "Little Brother," a comment that fuels Michigan

State to this day. He told the Detroit Free Press after Michigan's come from behind 28-24 victory:

"Sometimes, you get your little brother excited when you're playing basketball – let them get the lead, and then you comeback."

I of course spent years experiencing that very thing in the driveway with my Spartan brother Mark, but many felt the comment to be completely unnecessary, and Hart was ridiculed in the media.

Michigan lost to ohio state again in 2007, but eventually would end up in the Capital One Bowl, which they won 41-35 over Florida and their Heisman winner Tim Tebow and Head Coach Urban Meyer. The game would be the last that Lloyd Carr would coach at the University of Michigan. He had announced his retirement prior to the game. Mike Hart ran for 129 yards and two touchdowns on the day to close out his career at Michigan.

Mike Hart is one of the greatest backs ever to carry the ball at Michigan. Packed into his frame was a unique blend of power and quickness. He was a leader, incredibly competitive, and a **MICHIGAN MAN** through and through. Hart represented one of the *"THREE MICHIGAN HEISMAN CRITERIA."* His high school numbers and credentials spoke for themselves, but he was from New York and went 0-4 against the rival buckeyes. Mike Hart is still Michigan's career rushing leader with 5,040 yards rushing.

This Michigan great moved onto the NFL in 2008 when he was drafted by the Indianapolis Colts. He was still on the Colt's practice squad in 2010, after being waived on two occasions, but was no longer in the NFL for the 2011 season. He has rushed for 264 yards and scored two touchdowns in his NFL career. Hart remains involved with Michigan events, but his last trip to the Big House was as an Eastern Michigan assistant under Ron English. Hart even managed to excite the media prior to the matchup in 2011 when he said, *"I don't cheer for Michigan ever anymore. I watch the game and I watch as a coach trying to see what they're going to do."* Sometimes Hart's comments are a little hard to figure out. My parents met at Eastern, but come on **MICHIGAN MAN,** you know you are Blue at Hart. #20 was a Wolverine great.

2010, DENARD ROBINSON # 16

Denard Xavier Robinson arrived at Michigan in 2009. He arrived with plenty of hype. He was rated the #7 athlete in the country according to ESPN, but Michigan coach Rich Rodriguez and his staff had a unique angle. They told Robinson that if he came to Michigan, he would be given the opportunity to compete at quarterback, while most schools were already slating him at other positions. So think what you want about Rodriguez and his era at Michigan, but some creative recruiting and an offensive philosophy that was suited to Robinson's skills brought "Shoelace" to Ann Arbor. Oh yeah, that's right, this guy even arrived with a nickname. Robinson doesn't tie his cleats, utilizing only the Velcro to keep them on his incredibly fleet feet. When I say fleet, I mean really fleet. His recruiting reports listed this quarterback with 4.44 speed, and that must have been in golf shoes or flip flops.

When Robinson arrived for camp prior to the 2009 season, he was already facing an uphill battle at quarterback. Tate Forcier had graduated high school early and arrived in the spring. Most knew he had already seized the Michigan starting quarterback position. Denard had a lot to learn, and Forcier was the talk of the spring game. The offense was complicated, and Robinson was coming from a high school that had a play called "run around and stuff" to utilize his skills. Things went as expected, and Forcier was under, or I mean, behind the center due to Michigan's spread offense when Western Michigan came to town to open the season. Although he wasn't the starter, Michigan's staff would find ways to get Robinson on the field throughout his freshman season. On his very first collegiate snap, "Shoelace" ran right out of the shotgun formation after dropping the snap, eluded defenders, and raced 43 yards for a touchdown. Man is that guy fast I remember thinking. Michigan got off to a 4-0 start, and Robinson was providing plenty of highlights spelling Tate Forcier. The young Wolverines struggled through the Big Ten and finished 5-7 in 2009. Robinson started only once, and it wasn't at quarterback. Robinson lined up at running back to start the Wisconsin game in 2009. He finished his freshman campaign with 351 yards rushing and 5 touchdowns. He also contributed 188 yards passing with 2 touchdowns, and 4 interceptions serving as Forcier's backup.

Undeterred, Robinson spent the offseason getting better. Michigan was under investigation for NCAA sanctions related to excessive practice time under Coach Rich Rodriquez and his staff. Most were expecting a position change for Robinson, with Forcier the likely quarterback of the Wolverines. Robinson kept working. He would establish himself as a team leader, and was organizing many of the team unofficial workouts during the offseason. TOTALLY VOLUNTARY workouts☺ Forcier was struggling academically and rarely attended workouts. Robinson seized the opportunity.

Also during the offseason, Robinson would compete for Michigan on the track team. He won the 60 meter dash in his college track debut against you guessed it, ohio state. This guy wasn't fast for a quarterback, he was just fast. When preseason practices started in the summer of 2010, a much improved Denard Robinson was the talk of the Wolverines. The media wondered what would happen, but Robinson left that to the media. He kept working. No one doubted Robinson's incredible athleticism, but they did question his ability to pass and his overall intangibles.

As a lifetime Michigan fan, I was excited about the competition. As the story unfolded, I thought back to all the times that dual threat quarterbacks had come to the Big House and broke all of our hearts. Ricky Foggie, Johnny Johnson, Donovon McNabb, Armanti Edwards, the list goes on and on. Rodriquez was running a much different offense than past Michigan teams, and I couldn't help but think, "If you can't beat em, join em" as I got ready to cheer on the Wolverines in 2010. The question about the Michigan quarterback situation was answered when the University of Connecticut arrived at the Big House for the opening game of 2010.

Rodriguez kept his quarterback decision as a competitive advantage until the night before the game. "Shoelace" would make his debut against the Huskies as a starting quarterback and the team's first option on offense. Robinson would account for 383 yards of total offense in his first game as Michigan's starting quarterback. He had 197 yards rushing and 186 yards passing. Both his rushing display, and total offense numbers were Michigan records. Things were different in Ann Arbor, and Robinson's debut was the talk of the Big Ten.

The following week, Robinson put on a National display. Michigan's second game was at Notre Dame on NBC. The game was played on September 11th, 2010, and Notre Dame and Michigan were both honoring our great country, as well as the events that ensued ten years prior. Tom Harmon would surely have been proud of what #16 would do on the day. Robinson led Michigan to a come from behind 28-24 victory at Notre Dame. The numbers were staggering. **258 yards rushing and 244 yards passing**

in the game. In the first half, Robinson raced through the entire Notre Dame defense for an 87 yard touchdown. Quarterbacks aren't supposed to run like that. During the game he broke his own Michigan total offense in a game record, and this time, showcased some intangibles. Robinson led a 12 play, 72 yard drive that ended with touchdown run by the Michigan quarterback that gave them the win with 27 seconds remaining. "Shoelace" had arrived on the National College Football scene.

Robinson and the Wolverines continued to impress in victories over Bowling Green State University and the University of Massachusetts, and his numbers were unreal once again. He was compared to everybody from Rodriquez's former quarterback at West Virginia, Pat White to Barry Sanders. Any comparison seemed crazy to me though, this guy is unique. At Indiana, Robinson had 305 total yards of offense at HALFTIME, to include a 72 yard touchdown run on Michigan's 2nd offensive play of the game. He would finish the game with 494 yards of total offense and led Michigan to another victory. "Shoelace" was putting up video game numbers, and was at the top of most early season Heisman lists.

I told you that it isn't about the Heisman at Michigan, and with Denard, it was no different. His early season numbers were amazing, but Michigan really hadn't played anybody yet. They entered the meat of the 2010 schedule 5-0 with a Heisman front runner, but there were still plenty of questions about this Michigan TEAM. The defense hadn't shown the improvement that Michigan faithful were hoping for, and on special teams Michigan could barely kick an extra point, much less a field goal. Michigan State came to the Big House on October 9th, 2010 and defeated the Wolverines 34-17. Spartan running backs gashed through the Michigan defense, and MSU was able to control the ball and keep Denard Robinson and the offense on the sideline. It was a formula that the rest of the Big Ten would execute, and Michigan had few answers.

The Hawkeyes came to Ann Arbor the following week. Robinson would be injured in the game, and Tate Forcier came off the bench to bring Michigan back. He threw a 45 yard touchdown pass to Junior Hemingway, and scored on a 3 yard run. Iowa responded and ultimately won 38-28. Once again, Michigan's defense couldn't get off the field. One or two critical stops could have won the game for the Wolverines, but they couldn't do it. The following week Michigan traveled to Penn State. Robinson ran for 191 yards, but his play would again be overshadowed by the final score of 41-31 Penn State.

Michigan would win only one more game in 2010. They beat Illinois in a triple overtime thriller, but lost handily to ohio state and Mississippi State in the Gator Bowl.

Robinson finished 6th in the Heisman race, most of the votes surely coming from his early season performances.

2010 HEISMAN TROPHY VOTING RESULTS

PLACE	NAME	SCHOOL	CLASS	POSITION	1	2	3	TOTAL
1	CAM NEWTON	AUBURN	JR.	QB	729	24	28	2263
2	ANDREW LUCK	STANFORD	SO.	QB	78	309	227	1079
3	LAMICHAEL JAMES	OREGON	SO.	RB	22	313	224	916
4	KELLEN MOORE	BOISE STATE	JR.	QB	40	165	185	635
5	JUSTIN BLACKMON	OKLAHOMA ST.	SO.	WR	1	23	56	105
6	DENARD ROBINSON*	MICHIGAN	SO.	QB	6	16	34	84
7	RYAN MALLETT	ARKANSAS	JR.	QB	0	11	19	41
8	COLIN KAEPERNICK	NEVADA	SR.	QB	0	7	17	31
9	ANDY DALTON	TCU	SR.	QB	4	3	12	30
10	OWEN MARECIC	STANFORD	SR.	RB	3	1	5	16

"Shoelace" re-wrote the Michigan record book in 2010. He passed for 2,570 yards with 18 touchdowns and 11 interceptions. On the ground, Robinson's 1,702 yards and 14 touchdowns was not only the 4th greatest total in Michigan history, but the NCAA record for a quarterback. He was the first player in NCAA history to run and pass for over 1,500 yards, and his Michigan total offense in a season record was 1,032 yards better than the previous record set by John Navarre in 2003. Robinson was in the news following the 2010 season when a certain Heisman Trophy winner from Michigan referenced #16 while speaking at the Black Coaches and Administrators Conference in St. Petersburg, Florida. #21 Desmond Howard spoke boldly about Denard Robinson, and how he wasn't bigger than the program, Michigan, or all the other events surrounding Michigan in the offseason following 2010. The media received the comments as anti-Robinson, but that wasn't what Howard was going for. Yes, he was stating that Robinson wasn't bigger than Michigan. He made it clear, referencing the great Bo Schembechler that no man was bigger than the program. Howard was referencing the fact that when Rich Rodriquez was fired, and the initial media reaction was about whether or not Robinson would transfer. Howard pointed out that Denard Robinson was yet to win "anything," construed as a Big Ten Title, or National Championship, and the media roared that Desmond was bashing Denard. A week later, Desmond Howard clarified his comments, and even posted a picture and "tweeted" that he and Denard were fine, and that both were "Blue for Life."

This was just one specific example of what Denard Robinson's previous accomplishments and overall talents are causing throughout College Football. Denard Robinson opened 2011 as a Heisman Trophy Candidate. To be honest, why not? He is an incredible talent. He may be the fastest player in the B1G or however they portray it now. I didn't say the fastest quarterback, I said fastest player. There is no denying it. There were also, however, more questions surrounding Robinson than any other returning Heisman vote getter from 2010 when 2011 began. He was tailor made for Rich Rod's spread option offense, almost like it was designed for his skills. In 2011, Robinson found himself in a pro-style offense led by Al Borges and Brady Hoke. The adjustment period will continue in 2012.

In 2010, under Rich Rodriquez, there was immense pressure on Robinson and the offense to score nearly every time they had the ball. Defensive stops were few and far between. There was also several times when Michigan went for it on 4th down based on no faith in the kicking unit. Michigan's kickers were 4/14 on field goals in 2010. On plays where 3 points are usually at least a 60% chance, Michigan was going for it. The defense was usually ready, and got the ball back from the Wolverines.

The 2011 season was up and down for Denard Xavier Robinson. The offense was a mixture of a traditional, MICHIGAN, pro-style offense with elements of the spread that Al Borges and Brady Hoke simply couldn't help but to use. The challenge has been to refine Robinson's skills while maintaining the very things that had him on all the preseason Heisman Trophy lists. After a rain shortened week one victory over a capable Western Michigan Bronco's team Shoelace and Michigan added another miracle finish to the Michigan vs. Notre Dame rivalry in 2011.

During the first ever night game in Michigan Stadium's famed history Robinson and the Wolverines struggled throughout the first half. Notre Dame moved the ball at will, and Denard was turning the ball over. I remember my Dad calling and commenting that "you can't turn a thoroughbred into a plow horse" and that the pro-style Denard experiment was not working. He was right. The early season adjustment pains went on for weeks. In the second half against Notre Dame however, old Shoelace led an improbable Michigan comeback. After halftime, on a designed quarterback run, Robinson gained 39 yards dragging Notre Dame defenders until they finally got him to the ground. It was almost as if that play announced that Michigan wasn't going to go down easily in the Big House. I'll never know what the official adjustments or game plans were for the second half, but the ball was in Robinson's hands and with a little bit of "run around and stuff" and he would continue to make plays. Although he threw his 3rd interception after halftime, #16 brought the Wolverines back. The Wolverines scored on a touchdown pass from Robinson to Vincent Smith with 1:12 remaining in the game. As #16 and the offense went to the sideline, they thought surely that was enough.

Not quite. Notre Dame moved the ball down the field and with 30 seconds left in the game, the Irish took the lead on a 29 yard pass from Tommy Rees to Theo Riddick. The Big House went silent, and it was up to #16 to pull off another Big House Miracle. Robinson had burned the Irish the year before, winning the game on a late drive during his 502 yard outburst. Surely it couldn't happen again right? With 30 seconds left, Michigan was down by 3 and 80 long yards from the goal line. They needed a miracle to even get into field goal range, and with the kicking woes from 2010, would that even help? Robinson's first pass sailed out of bounds. Then on a second down, Robinson escaped the pocket and laid a perfect pass in the hands of Jeremy Gallon, escaping Irish defenders and throwing on the run. The defenders took the wrong angles to Gallon who was able to escape, cut across the field, and finally get out of bounds at the Irish16 yard line. Gallon caught the pass on the right sideline and finally stopped the clock all the way across the field. Shoelace and Michigan were in business once again. While the announcers talked about a field goal, Michigan lined up for a play. Robinson threw a fade route to the right side of the end zone and Roy Roundtree went up and caught it. After a review that seemed to take years, the touchdown was confirmed and Brent Musburger of ABC/ESPN proclaimed Denard Robinson was the most exciting player in College Football. Michigan prevailed 35-31. Although Robinson did not surpass his 2010 Total against Notre Dame he did have 446 total yards and accounted for 5 touchdowns. Vintage Shoelace.

Robinson spent the remainder of 2011 adjusting to the pro-style offense. Both he and the new coaching staff were learning each week, and working on the discipline versus unique abilities balance for #16. The season consisted of intense scrutiny for Robinson on a weekly basis.

His passing numbers were up and down while backup quarterback Devin Gardner saw action in several games with Robinson on the field or not. Michigan lost games to Michigan State and Iowa. Both were close. Costly interceptions and some play calling left many Michigan fans scratching their heads. Some were calling for Gardner, and once again a position change for Shoelace. The media gave the issues more attention than they probably deserved, but that is what happens when you are the coaches or the quarterback on the team with the most wins in the history of College Football. Through it all, Robinson and the Wolverines bounced back and finished the regular season strong.

Michigan, despite all the concerns about Robinson and the offense, proved they were a much better **TEAM** in 2011. As Shoelace slowly fell out of the Heisman race, Michigan was winning and proving that their leader and most dynamic talent didn't need to produce 500 yards of offense each week. Fitzgerald Toussaint emerged at running back, and the two would become the first tandem since Rob Lytle and Gordon Bell to each surpass 1,000 yards in the same season. Robinson ran for 1,163 yards in 2011, and Fitzgerald Toussaint had 1,011. Robinson was all smiles while falling out of the race as this team improved. Sounds a lot like Bo doesn't it? The defense improved, and I mean dynamically as the season wore on. Once the unit of concern, the defense was putting Michigan in position to win each week.

For the final two regular season games 0f 2011, Michigan and Denard Robinson figured out a balance that will prove to be lethal in 2012. Michigan played Nebraska in the Big House on November 19th, 2011, and won 45-17. What I remember most from the game was the comments from the ESPN team covering the game. Included were buckeye great Chris Speilman and soon to be at the time, buckeye coach Urban Meyer. I had to laugh as the two professionals reiterated the conversation that my father and I had been having for two months. Sometimes we armchair quarterbacks get it right. The discussion was about Denard of course, and how he could be the most dangerous. As fast and as prolific a runner Robinson is, rarely did he scramble for yards. Under Rodriquez and now Hoke /Al Borges, Robinson is the primary running threat. However, most of those runs since Shoelace arrived in the Big Ten have been designed. Based on coaching, his desire to do what he has been told to do, or the overall process adjusting to the offensive scheme it was incredibly rare that #16 would drop back to pass and run when opportunities were there. The improv skills that made guys like Jim Harbaugh, Vince Young, and others so dangerous found their way to the Big House on November 19th, 2011. So as Urban Meyer and Chris Speilman drove the point home, I sat back with a smile as Robinson responded. Apparently a light bulb went off, maybe Borges had been preaching the same lesson, but all of the sudden, he was expanding his game to another level that defensive coordinators will lose even more sleep over if that is possible.

Against Nebraska and ohio state a healthy #16 would give two good defenses fits. Hoke brought further light to Robinson's injuries in 2011 that ranged from a staph infection to bruised ribs. He had a bad wrist as well as a hand injury. During the season Hoke never brought it up, and #16? He just played. On November 19th, the newly true dual threat quarterback completed 11/18 passes for 180 yards and two touchdowns. Denard the scrambler ran for 83 yards and two more touchdowns. He displayed control of the game plan and this **MICHIGAN MAN** led his **TEAM** to a 45-17 victory. Oh yes the buckeyes were up next.

On November 26th, 2011, Robinson picked up where he left off against Nebraska. Michigan hadn't beaten osu since 2003, and of all Robinson has done at Michigan, that DNA required to beat the ohio school had been missing. Their arch rival was in the midst of a disappointing season and came to the Big House with a 6-5 record based on a coaching change, suspensions, and the learning curve of a true freshman quarterback. Despite it all, it's still **THE GAME** for a reason, and instant classic was about to be born. Shoelace and Braxton Miller would put on a show that only two athletes of their caliber can put on. The game took me back to the previous chapters of this story when matchups like Woodson vs Boston, Griffith vs Gordon Bell, and Desmond against everybody made the rivalry what it is today. Michigan prevailed 40-34 as Denard Xavier Robinson ran for 170 yards and two touchdowns while completing 14/17 passes for 167 yards and 3 more touchdowns. The buckeye's freshman didn't back down and passed for 235 yards and two touchdowns while rushing for 100 yards and scoring once on the ground. Certainly the Big Ten and and other 2012 opponents preparing for these two dual threat quarterbacks right now. I hope Miller doesn't like tattoos for the sake of buckeye fans, but under the new coach, I don't think it will be a problem. It's starting to feel like the old days again. I think another Michigan vs osu, Big Ten and Heisman Race, is set for 2012 whether it is the goal or not.

As far as the *"THREE MICHIGAN HEISMAN CRITERIA"* go, Robinson has some work to do. He is a mega recruit with blazing speed and athleticism. Coming from Deerfield Beach, Florida, you could even stretch to say that he is from enemy territory if Michigan plans to compete for a National Championship in 2012. They also have bowl wins over Florida in 2003 and 2008, and the rivalry may be growing. Urban Meyer even once recruited Mr. Robinson, but next fall, he will be coaching the ohio state university as they call it. Despite losing his first two contests against ohio state handily, things turned around in 2011. This guy has now brought it home against the buckeyes and will look to do it again in 2012. If Robinson does find a way to join Harmon, Howard, and Woodson it certainly won't be the goal for the Wolverines. In 2012 the door is open for Shoelace to have his greatest season yet for the Wolverines. He had a Sugar Bowl that reflected the season, some ups, some downs, but in the end a Wolverine victory. Michigan has also abandoned the directional Michigan opener for 2012. Shoelace and the Wolverines are taking on Alabama and somewhere Bo is smiling.

Unless Rich Rod and his famed "snake oil" somehow lure #16 to the desert, it's hard to imagine Robinson not being in New York in early December 2012, playing within the confines of a Michigan **TEAM.** I'm not really that worried about Rich Rod, Robinson is a **MICHIGAN MAN** through and through. Heisman or not, check out the Michigan Football Record Book, his name can be found throughout. The 2011 Heisman went to Robert Griffin III of Baylor, a dual threat quarterback, team leader, and game breaker. Griffin is WAY too fast to be at that position like Robinson. Maybe we'll see the same in 2012. It won't be the goal, but Shoelace can play, and with another offseason to improve Robinson and the Wolverines will be a force to be reckoned with in 2012....98-21-2...**16?**

MICHIGAN AGAIN...MICHIGAN

So as Michigan entered the 2011 season, there were far more questions than answers like in 1969, 2008, 2009, and 2010. The good news is 2011 was about some greatly missed MICHIGAN football. This story, told through some amazing individuals has outlined some of the greatest seasons and performances in Michigan's great history. It is told through the Heisman Trophy, which wasn't, isn't, and will never be the goal during any given season. No matter what anyone says outside of this proud University to include me, it won't be. Not only does Michigan not promote the Heisman, as outlined throughout this story, but they have also been addressing much bigger issues and getting back to Michigan Football. This book has outlined the three players who have won the Heisman Memorial Trophy as well as those who have finished in the Top Ten voting since 1940. One common thread through it all is that each of these men performed at a high level and led Michigan TEAMS to successful seasons. Head Coach Brady Hoke took over a Michigan team that finished 7-6 in 2010, as well as one that hadn't won a bowl game since the 2008 Capital One Bowl over Tim Tebow and Florida. Hoke is a **MICHIGAN MAN** who was an Assistant Coach under Lloyd Carr from 1995-2002. He was around when

Biakabutuka and company ruined the buckeyes season. He contributed to the National Championship in 1997. He gets it. As I researched for this book and watched games from those great years, there was Hoke. Energetic, tough, and

most memorably finding Charles Woodson on the bench after the amazing one handed interception at Michigan State. He was there. Also during his time as an assistant, he often traveled down the hall to gain insight from none other than the late Bo Schembechler. The man who now leads the Wolverines declared publicly, even to his former employer, that he wanted to coach Michigan. Even that he would have, "walked to Ann Arbor" to take the Michigan job. Now, he's got it, and it feels like Michigan again.

Before Hoke's hiring there was divided Michigan community and fan base. Most of 2009 and 2010, the media focused on whether or not Rich Rodriquez would be retained. Although each player carried themselves well for the most part, I am certain that the speculation had an impact on the team. Why wouldn't it? Worse yet, some of the most influential and most respected **MICHIGAN MEN** distanced themselves from the program during the Rodriguez era. For the first time in the Football Program's history there were significant allegations and penalties from the NCAA. It was one of the many factors that led to Hoke's dream job becoming available. Many fans wanted Harbaugh, but most also knew that he would ultimately land in the NFL. Although I grew up watching him play and have always been a Harbaugh fan, he wasn't what they needed and 2011 proved it all. Michigan needed Hoke. They needed someone like Bo, Moeller, and Carr. Someone who only knows of **ONE** team. A **MICHIGAN MAN** who plans on retiring a Wolverine. Some of the questions and issues seemed to be answered during Hoke's first press conference.

The Rodriquez era was marked with speculation, but he too had an uphill climb. His massive personnel overhaul and attempt to win in the B1G with the spread offense ultimately ran out of time. Michigan went 3-9, 5-7, and finally 7-6 in three years. Would there have been more wins for that staff with more time? Ultimately, it no longer matters. Rich Rod thought so, and even had the guts to say it. Really? Who baked what? Anyway, there have been some challenges for this new staff but so far so good for all of us that bleed blue.

I know anybody who reads this book already knows it, but I want to reiterate that **MICHIGAN, I SAID MICHIGAN, HAD NOT BEATEN** ohio state **SINCE 2003 until Brady Hoke arrived.** To put it in perspective, it had been 2926 days, 252,806,400 seconds, 70,224 hours, and oh yes 418 painful weeks. Not since Chris Perry and Braylon Edwards were slashing through the buckeye secondary, and Michigan defenders would leave the game with scarlet and gray all over their helmets. Unbelievable. That game is not only memorable for me because it was the last time the Wolverines came out on top until this year, but also because of where I watched it. My journey to follow the Wolverines hasn't always been as easy as it is today through the amazing industry that is College Football, and the media resources that support it. Have I mentioned High Definition television has surpassed the light bulb for the greatest invention ever for sports fans like me? It hasn't always been that easy for me.

In 2003, I watched that game in a place called Iraq. It was the same deployment I mentioned earlier in this story, but what I didn't mention was the Michigan victory over the ohio state university. My time at war began at invasion and went through the first year of this war (you know, the one that isn't even on TV anymore while guys like Harmon and Chappuis walk the alleys of Baghdad and the caves of Afghanistan to keep us all safe). It was like nothing I had ever done before, and I am thankful each day to be here and for those who continue the fight. By the time November came after months of bouncing from place to place, my unit was actually in a more built up area. We even had access to AFN (Armed Forces Network) that is like Directv for bad ass soldiers fighting for the USA. I watched some of a few games, but when it came time for the buckeyes I was ready to bring a little bit of home to our Battalion Staff. The project started two weeks earlier. The AFN was tied into an area that was somewhat like a break room, but that wasn't good enough for LT Gallagher. I purchased a longer coax cable from an Iraqi interpreter, and I mean longer. He haggled about price, but we finally got it done. Instead of going to bed that night, I started spreading the word. Game night was on in our TOC (Tactical Operations Center). The projector we used for our final mission briefs got hooked to the satellite dish, speakers were found, and guys were helping. The games over there don't start until around 11 based on the time difference, but there was no way I was sleeping.

Everything was great, and we all knew we would have a little piece of home on the big screen as long as John G, our commander didn't find out. He was a Ranger STUD, a great leader, and always focused on what we were there to do. I learned a lot from that man. I think we had seen the first Michigan score when he walked in, and I thought "OH S&%T." You have to understand that I was the

Communications Officer, and responsible for all such equipment. It wasn't exactly official business to anybody but me! He and I also had a Schembechler and Harbaugh kind of relationship, so I braced for what would come. *"WHAT THE HELL GALLAGHER?"* Then he smiled and asked if we had seen the Virginia score. He was in too, and the Wolverines provided another lift to us all and a little piece of home.

I can tell you that I will never forget that game, the guys I watched it with, or the results. I will also tell you that I am out now, and I wasn't planning on going back to War to see Michigan beat the buckeyes. Good news, Coach Hoke and the Wolverines already made it happen. This Coach referred to their rival as the "ohio school" from day one. He put a countdown clock on the wall. I will never forget the 2011 game either, watching it with my wife and her family as if some great quest had been completed. It had been a long time, but now the Wolverines go back to work. Even with a BCS Bowl victory, there are still four straight losses to the Spartans and plenty of work to be done in Ann Arbor. Nobody knows that better than Brady Hoke.

Sports are one of the many things that make this country great. Teams, moments, games, they have an ability to lift the spirits of a stadium, arena, city, state, and even nation. As a proud Michigander, I am not crazy enough to think that everybody cheers for Michigan. I get it. I do know however that the State of Michigan has faced some tough, tough, times. Sports have always been able to lift the spirits of a proud state that has seen jobs leave and an economy hit harder than most. For the past several years it was up to the Spartans, Tigers, and Red Wings to provide Michigan with those moments and the sense of pride that is desperately needed.

I have family and friends toughing it out in my home state. They are people who are being forced to learn new skills and begin new careers. Sounds like a certain team, doesn't it? It has been great to see the Wolverines get back into the equation of elevating some spirits. They have the right people in place, and it's time to draw on the great tradition. Athletic Director, David Brandon, took his time evaluating what was wrong with the Wolverines and he fixed it. Brandon played for Bo. He hired another **MICHIGAN MAN.** Brady Hoke is the guy to do it and the revival is off to a great start. Look back at the stories outlined in this book and if you bleed BLUE like me, enjoy it. The Heisman is just one of those many traditions and I'm not promoting it. I will also tell you that if Robinson or anyone else is in the equation the Wolverines will be in a much better state than they have been in for several years. This program has won 72% of its' games over the years. The seasons outlined in this story, with Heisman contenders playing within the confines of the team have seen Michigan win 79% of the time. Nope, it's not about the Heisman, but it is definitely an indicator of team success. You won't hear the word "rebuilding" out of Brady Hoke. You won't hear about "his guys." Yes it's a transition, but from day one he said only one thing, **"THIS IS MICHIGAN."** In the years to come, I look forward to that truth. Maybe I care too much about games I watch on TV, but if you are reading this, than I am probably not alone. It's a family tradition and part of who I am. With some great coaching, *COACH OF THE YEAR* coaching, responsive players, and a little luck they will be back to a Championship sooner than you think. Somewhere Bo Schembechler will be smiling and

IT WILL BE MICHIGAN AGAIN...

MICHIGAN

INDEX / HEISMAN PERFORMANCE

MICHIGAN HEISMAN PERFORMANCE RATING = % OF VOTES / HEISMAN VOTING PLACE

RANKING THESE 21 MICHIGAN GREATS....

RANKING	NAME	POSITION	JERSEY #	RATING	PAGE #
1	TOM HARMON	HB/DB/K/P	98	0.5424	14
2	DESMOND HOWARD	WR/KR	21	0.5048	76
3	CHARLES WOODSON	CB/WR/KR	2	0.3859	137
4	BOB CHAPPUIS	HB	49	0.139	31
5	TYRONE WHEATLEY	RB	6	0.0671	119
6	JIM HARBAUGH	QB	4	0.0345	63
7	RICK LEACH	QB	7	0.0314	56
8	ROB LYTLE	RB	41	0.0284	52
9	BOB TIMBERLAKE	QB	28	0.0233	38
10	CHRIS PERRY	RB	23	0.0192	168
11	MIKE HART	RB	20	0.0165	188
12	RON KRAMER	TE/DE	87	0.0152	35
13	ANTHONY CARTER	WR/KR	1	0.0083	59
14	BOB WESTFALL	FB/LB	86	0.0076	26
15	BILL DALEY	FB	45	0.0072	29
16	RON JOHNSON	RB	40	0.0049	41
17	DENNIS FRANKLIN	QB	9	0.004	44
18	DENARD ROBINSON	QB	16	0.0026	204
19	GORDON BELL	RB	5	0.0023	48
20	BRAYLON EDWARDS	WR/KR	1	0.0013	176
21	TIM BIAKABUTUKA	RB	21	0.0008	130

ABOUT THE AUTHOR

In case you missed it in the story, my name is Martin Gallagher, and I have a little blue in my blood. I give my Dad the credit, and spent some great years in Ann Arbor growing up living about 3 miles from Michigan Stadium. I have been a fan as long as I can remember, and my mom thinks it was even before that.

Although I am a Michigan fan, I'm certainly an educated one. I remember a movie that came out in 1993 called Sniper. It wasn't a great movie, but it did have Tom Berenger. Before he enters the jungle with the new guy played by Billy Zane, he says something to the effect of ***"What I know about this jungle son, is that I'm it."*** That's me, although I watch every Michigan game, it doesn't stop there. What I know about Michigan is that I'm in it. The digital world is amazing. I am able to follow this team on a daily basis. This story has been in my head for at least ten years, and in March 2011, my Dad and I decided it was time to tell it. We were both writing, and the Michigan world will also hear from him **SOON.** From the first time I watched a game with my wife she could tell it was serious. I told her that Michigan brings the people together, and at our house it is usually an event. We live in North Carolina, but every Saturday I pull out the lucky jerseys, we make food, and people walk through the door. I have converted many to love the Wolverines, but more than anything it is like being home.

I have a wonderful career in Construction Management, but I feel passion is something you have to live. Whatever you love, whatever you like, and whatever you do when nobody is looking could very well be your greatest opportunity. I've never worked harder in my career, things are wild. For awhile I was working in 4 different cities, and what I have learned through this process is that you can't wait for the "Right Time" to do anything. It may never come. So I stayed up late, fell asleep at the computer, invested in 5 Hour Energy, and pulled out the VHS tapes. If you are motivated, you can get a lot done while others are sleeping. I hope you have enjoyed these amazing stories and memories. I hope that

they elevate excitement for everyone with Blue in their blood pulling for this team like me. My journey continues in 2012 following the Sugar Bowl win, a game I watched with my in laws

while talking with my family near and far. There were some serious ties to both Michigan and Virginia Tech, two teams that had amazingly never played. The magic of this sport never ceases to amaze me. Dad, fun project, thanks for the support. To the **MICHIGAN MEN** who made this story over the years, thanks for the memories. I'll see you at the **BIG HOUSE!**

Made in the USA
Charleston, SC
18 August 2012